The Springer Series on Death and Suicide

ROBERT KASTENBAUM, Ph.D., Series Editor

Lisl Marburg Goodman, Ph.D. is an associate professor of psychology at Jersey City State College and senior clinical psychologist at the Psychiatric Services Center in White Plains, New York. She received her Ph.D. from the New School for Social Research. Dr. Goodman has published articles in personality research and thanatology in scientific journals and she has participated in symposia and paper sessions at major psychological conventions in the United States and in Europe. Thanatology has been her special area of interest since 1971, when she devised one of the earliest college courses in that field for Jersey City State College.

DEATH AND THE CREATIVE LIFE

Conversations with Prominent
Artists and Scientists

Lisl Marburg Goodman, PH.D.

Springer Publishing Company
New York

To the Colonel

Appreciation is acknowledged to Professor Walter Kaufmann for permission to reproduce his translation of Hölderlin's poem "Nur einen Sommer" from Walter Kaufmann, *Existentialism, Religion, and Death,* New American Library, © 1976 by Walter Kaufmann.

Springer Publishing Company, Inc.
200 Park Avenue South
New York, New York   10003

81 82 83 84 85 / 10 9 8 7 6 5 4 3 2 1

Library of Congress Cataloging in Publication Data
Goodman, Lisl Marburg.
  Death and the creative life.

  (Springer series on death and suicide; 4)
  Bibliography: p.
  Includes index.
    1. Death—Addresses, essays, lectures.   2. Life—
Addresses, essays, lectures.   3. Artists—United States—
Interviews.   4. Scientists—United States—Interviews.
I. Title.   II. Series. [DNLM: 1. Achievement.   2. Attitude to death.   3. Creativeness. W1 SP685P v. 4 /BF 789.
D4 G653d]
BD444.G66   128'.5   81-1045
ISBN 0-8261-3500-5
ISBN 0-8261-3501-3 (pbk.)

Printed in the United States of America

Contents

Part III   WINNING THE RACE WITH DEATH

Foreword

The symphony that Mozart composed when he was deathly ill is seldom heard these days because he recovered, matured, and created other orchestral works of greater stature. Yet, this symphony is serenity itself. Who would have known the child composer was feverish, and death a close prospect? The Concerto for Orchestra that Bela Bartok composed two centuries later has sweep, power and wit. Where is the leukemia that was draining Bartok's life? Where are the somber rumblings of death?

The artistic response to death is not always what one might predict. The same may be said for the scientist's response to death. When an astro-physicist plants a seedling, does his time perspective force him to think of our no-future planet—and, if so, does he go ahead and plant the seedling anyhow? What does the psychologist make of a developmental process through which some people grow wiser and more resourceful with age while their bodies bow to the heralds of death?

Artists and scientists are not alone in their personal encounters with mortality. But death is likely to be viewed differently by the individual whose life is devoted to creation. Does the creative process somehow dull the sting of death or postpone death? Or, is the chill on-rush of time even more a menace to the person who has creations as well as flesh at stake?

If questions of this sort interest you, then you will be impatient to proceed to the interviews and interpretations offered to us by Lisl Goodman. This book takes us into a realm that has been surprisingly neglected by the death awareness movement. You may or may not agree with Dr. Goodman's specific interpretations, but I am confident that you will share my gratitude to her for taking us somewhere we have not been before—inside the minds of distinguished artists and scientists of our own time as they reflect on life and death.

Robert Kastenbaum, Ph.D.

Preface

Hypotheses grow out of introspection; at least with me they do. Since childhood I have been plagued by the idea of death approaching in Juggernaut fashion with no possibility of escape. I remember sitting on the floor with my building blocks as I thought that if only I could put up a structure—something that has never been built before—I would have the solution for preventing death. The idea of building or creating something special remained *the* solution, but eventually it changed to a less radical one. It no longer demanded the abolition of death; rather, by making something special of one's life, death could be changed from a catastrophic to a desirable end.

Now the unbearable thought was of being cut off from life *before . . . Before* stood for all the things I wanted to do, I wanted to see, I wanted to experience—not just once but over and over again up until the time when I would not want to experience them any longer. Suddenly the solution seemed so simple; if one does all one is capable of doing and all one wants to do until one has *spent* oneself, death would represent the *goal* of a completed life.

In English we lack the word for the very expressive German *vollenden*. Indeed, saying that someone is "bringing his/her life to completion" (a translation of *sein Leben vollenden*) sounds rather awkward. Interestingly, when one speaks of someone ending his or her life—using the active rather than the passive voice—it connotes suicide. We rarely think of people actively engaged in completing their lives. This does not mean that we are not striving toward completion; we are just not fully aware of it—we have not postulated it as a goal. But how does one complete life? Perhaps the answer is in self-actualization in the most literal sense. Yet self-actualization has suffered from misuse. When members of the "Me" generation speak of self-identity, self-awareness, and self-actualization, they really mean self-centered indulgence in anything that seems advantageous to "number one." In this book self-actualization refers to the conversion of one's possibilities into actualities: it means giving form, expression, and structure to one's potentials. If we were to succeed in actualizing all our potentials, we would really be bringing life to its natural end. Life, then, would truly be completed. I believe that this is where the solution to my childhood quest rests. My aim in writing this book was to probe the feelings and thoughts about death of a few highly self-actualized individuals and to shed some light on the relationship between one's level of self-actualization and one's attitude toward death.

Acknowledgments

First and foremost, my thanks go to all the interviewees who were willing to probe into so personal a subject matter as death and to share their thoughts and feelings with me. I am especially grateful to Professor Howard Gruber and to Professor John Wheeler, who gave so generously of their time and their wisdom.

The ideas developed in this book have been influenced by innumerable writers—poets, philosophers, scientists—many of whom I cannot trace, most of them long dead. The thanatologists whose works have inspired me most directly are Kurt Eissler, Herman Feifel, and Robert Kastenbaum.

My very special thanks go to Professor Feifel and to Professor Kastenbaum for reading the entire manuscript and for their constructive criticism and warm encouragement.

My appreciation to Jeff Marburg-Goodman and Maria Di Santo for their help in organizing, editing, and typing the manuscript; to Linda Marks, Editor at Springer Publishing Co., for her cheerfulness and willingness to solve problems; to Lee Ann Hoff and Maryanne Vent for invaluable discussions and suggestions; to Ronald Marburg Goodman and to Krishnan for their help in enlisting scientists for the interviews, and finally, to my husband, Sam Goodman, for listening and participating in endless explorations of the topic of death, for being such a receptive sounding board, for his patience and love and encouragement.

Introduction

Tarry a while, O Death, I cannot die
With all my blossoming hopes unharvested,
My joys ungarnered, all my songs unsung,
And all my tears unshed.

Tarry awhile, till I am satisfied
Of love and grief, of earth and altering sky;
Till all my human hungers are fulfilled,
O Death, I cannot die!

—— *Sarojini Naidu*

The present book is the outcome of seven years of investigations, in the course of which my students and I have interviewed almost 700 people on their attitudes toward death.

From its very inception the entire study was based on the assumption that people are not afraid of death per se, but of the incompleteness of their lives, of dying prematurely, before they have had a chance to develop their talents, to actualize their potentials. A corollary to this assumption is that once one has succeeded in reaching self-fulfillment by giving form to all the latent possibilities within, death no longer presents a threat: one has won the race with death.

To determine whether or not people who have actualized their potentials to the utmost do indeed fear death less than those who have not, I have conducted interviews with individuals at different levels of self-actualization; from the foremost creative artists and scientists of our time, to abysmal failures who see their lives as wasted.

The twenty-two interviews with leading artists and scientists comprise the main body of this book.

The first obstacle in interviewing famous artists presented itself immediately: gaining access to them. Unaware, at first, that the topic to be discussed was too foreboding for most people (too foreboding to expose a spouse, friend, or a client to it), I had counted on several sources which could be helpful in making the necessary contacts. The first and most promising was a friend of mine, a well-known musicologist, author, and critic, who is in close daily contact with many great musicians. I intended to interview him first, hoping that if he found the whole procedure painless—perhaps even stimulating—he might be willing to help establish contact with some of his artist-friends. I made my first strategic mistake (followed by many more) when I called his home and explained to his wife what the intended interview was about; namely, that I was investigating the dimensions of phenomenal time perspectives, creative accomplishment, and attitudes toward death. After seconds of silence, she asked unbelievingly, "Attitudes toward what?"

"Death."

"D-E-A-T-H?"

"Yes, death."

"Well, that sounds very interesting; fascinating indeed! I would love to talk to you about it. Very interesting, *really*—but the problem is first of all, Max is very busy—terribly busy right now—and he is tense, very tense and nervous. I really worry that talking about death may depress him too much."

I tried to reassure her that such an interview would be likely to relieve rather than create tension. She asked, "Can you guarantee that he will not get upset?" Of course I could not. I explained that just walking into his office could upset him for one reason or another. But she decided that she would think it over, discuss it with her husband, and call me back. She never did.

The outcome of this first attempt at setting up an interview was a rather typical one, as I learned eventually. Months later, after having conducted many interviews, I had occasion to tell Max about them. He showed great interest and was eager to be interviewed. Like most people who participated, he did not feel that the interview was threatening or depressing; rather he enjoyed the experience. Unfortunately, he did not volunteer an introduction to any of his artist-friends.

Another interesting incident occurred in one of my seminars on death. Discussing the theoretical relationship between levels of creative accomplishment and fear of death, I remarked that attitudes toward death of great artists have, thus far, only been inferred from their works of art or from biographical or autobiographical notes. Most of these studies were done from a historical perspective; and I added, "If only one had access to highly accomplished, creative people such as Leonard Bernstein, one could investigate their attitude toward death firsthand."

One of my students asked whether I really wanted to interview famous artists; if so, she was sure that she could arrange interviews with Leonard Bernstein and Isaac Stern, who were both friends of her uncle, a well-known playwright. A few days later it seemed all set. Her uncle had agreed to ask his two friends for an interview with me. He suggested that I write a short note to each of them stating the purpose of the interview which he would personally deliver. My student thought that I should also request an interview with her uncle, "for the sake of his ego." However, when he read what the interviews were about, he balked. Death was too personal a matter; he could not approach his friends with such a request. He also felt that discussing such a topic could be damaging. On this occasion, as well as on several others, I came across the vague notion that this "morbid" topic could upset some precarious balance necessary for creative activity, as if the very thought of death introduced an idea both alien and inimical to their work.

I finally discovered that the only way to make contact with artists—especially performers—was to get to them directly, avoiding spouses, friends, and agents, who form a protective barrier around them. Whenever I succeeded in establishing direct contact by letter or by telephone, many of the artists showed interest and agreed to be interviewed.[1]

Although the scientists were generally on a more rigid schedule than the artists, it was far easier to obtain interviews with the former. They too were contacted by letter, or on some occasions personally, at their university or at a lecture. Their interviews tended to be shorter than those with artists, and there was little sidetracking from the main

---

[1] I am indebted to Robert Sherman, Program Director of WQXR, who advised me to obtain a copy of *Musical America*, a journal in which every performing artist is listed under his agent's name, and to address my letter to the respective artist, in care of his agency.

topic. No entertaining anecdotes and no drinks. Perhaps because of the greater adherence to the framework of the interview, specific questions were treated more thoroughly. But it was often harder to get at subjective experiences instead of intellectualizations.

Almost all the interviews were conducted at the scientists' offices, in contrast to the homes or hotel suites of artists. This more formal setting may have had some bearing on the stylistic differences. But there were other differences as well.

I faced the "famous people" interviews with certain preconceived ideas and some trepidation. When artists—mostly performing artists—agreed to an interview, there was no question in their minds or in mine that they were doing me a favor. However, scientists, no matter how prominent, seemed more concerned with the issues to be discussed than with their role as respondent. In fact, they frequently voiced their appreciation for having been contacted and for being included in the study. Even so, I felt much more at ease before an interview with an artist than before one with a scientist. I suppose I had taken for granted the artist's intimacy with death which is, after all, one of the major themes that finds expression in all artistic modalities. On the other hand, I had expected scientists to show reluctance to discuss so "slippery" a concept as death. Expression of one's innermost feelings is the essence of art, while almost the opposite can be said about the content of science. In the latter, ideal conditions supposedly require detachment rather than subjective involvement with the subject matter. Indeed, scientists have avoided death as a field of study as thoroughly as artists have made it one of their leitmotifs.

Thus, I had no doubt that the artists would freely discuss their thoughts and attitudes toward death. But I was apprehensive of the way "tough-minded" scientists would respond to questions concerning such an "unmeasurable," "untestable" concept as death.

Surprise! It was the artists who were most frequently reluctant to discuss their feelings about death, while a number of scientists became so involved with the topic that they suggested exploring the issues further. Indeed, some of them proposed follow-up interviews, while others elaborated on their views by letter.

The main concern of this book is to capture some of the highly idiosyncratic ways in which a few extraordinarily self-actualizing individuals confront crucial issues of life and death. However, to appreciate fully the qualitative differences in attitudes, their responses to specific questions are compared with those obtained from people on different levels of self-actualization. Unless otherwise indicated, all the comparisons made throughout the book are based on a study of 331 interviewees, classified into ten groups on the basis of age and level of self-actualization.[2] (Table 3-1 contains the description of the groups.) One hundred one young people between seventeen and thirty-four years old make up groups 1, 2 and 3, corresponding to high, medium, and low self-actualization; seventy adults from thirty-seven to seventy-three years of age make up groups 4, 5, and 6, corresponding again to high, medium, and low self-actualization levels. The only criteria used in the selection of 160 individuals (groups 7 through 10) were age and sex, with twenty males and twenty females in each of four age-groups. With levels of self-actualization randomly distributed throughout these four groups, they constitute a baseline or control, isolating the effect of age on the attitudes toward death.

Inclusion into high, medium, or low self-actualization categories was determined by objective and subjective criteria, such as academic achievements, outstanding creative accomplishments, socioeconomic levels, and the respondents' own perception of their accomplishments and their feelings of self-fulfillment.

More specifically, all the artists and scientists I interviewed (group 4)[3] had been evaluated by professionals or critics as prominent contributors to their field. An added requirement for the sculptors and painters was that they had works on permanent exhibition in reputable museums or galleries; musicians had to be presently performing as soloists in major concert halls here and abroad. Chronological age had not served as a factor in the selection process of this group, which was based solely on accomplishment criteria and availability. The fact that most of the artists and scientists I interviewed are middle-aged or above is simply a consequence of their level of accomplishment. There

[2]The results of this study have been presented at the XXIst International Congress of Psychology in Paris,.France, 1976. The study is listed under the title, Attitudes towards Death as a Function of Age and Level of Accomplishment in *Proceedings*, XXIst International Congress of Psychology, Presses Universitaires de France, 1978, p. 325. A summary of the presentation has been published in the *Abstract Guide*, French Society of Psychology, 1976, p. 318.

[3]The interviews with Eva Le Gallienne and with Karl Pribram were conducted at a later date. They are not included in group 4 (Table 3-1).

are very few *young* artists and scientists who rank among the top in their particular field, which was one of the criteria for selection.

However, chronological age was a factor in the selection of interviewees classified as "medium" on the self-actualization dimension (group 5). They were recruited from among professionals and executives, on the basis of closely matching the artist/scientist group on all but the creativity-accomplishment dimension.

Low levels of self-actualization are harder to assess, since subtle forms of self-fulfillment may be present in the absence of visible accomplishments. Thus, more stringent subjective criteria, in addition to the objective ones, had to be met for inclusion into the "low" self-actualization groups (groups 3 and 6). The objective criteria were of the order of chronic unemployment, drifting without any vocational preference, welfare recipience, abuse of drugs or alcohol. Subjective criteria were based on expressions of dissatisfaction and helplessness such as "life has passed me by," "my life has been wasted," "I never had a chance," among others. Age is the only factor which differentiates the two "low" self-actualization groups.

The young adults classified into the high or the medium self-actualization group consisted of college students. Inclusion into one of the two groups (1 or 2) was based on achievements, goal-directedness, and the degree of satisfaction with present and projected accomplishments and life-styles.

Attitudes toward death were assessed on a conscious and on a fantasy level by individual, in-depth, semistructured interviews, guided by an interview schedule devised by the author. The entire procedure of the interviews, with the questions and the rationale of the Standard Interview Schedule, is described in chapter 3.

However, the data obtained from the 160 respondents, designated here as control groups (7 through 10), followed a different procedure. The interviewees, approached in shopping centers, hotel lobbies, department stores, air terminals, and train stations, were asked only the key questions of the Standard Interview Schedule.

Some of the limitations in the scope of individual selection need to be mentioned:

1. Performing musicians predominated in the artists' group. This fact can be ascribed to some practical considerations as well as to

intuitive ones. Let us discuss the latter first. The performing artist's experience of self-fulfillment must be encapsulated in moments of extraordinary performances. There is no chance for rewriting, erasing, or contemplating the product. The absolute peak experiences occur at the moment of being artistically engaged, with the added effect of the adulation of the audience—the effect of applause. All this may very well maximize the subjective experience of self-actualization and thus sharpen the focus of our study. The more concrete considerations arose in terms of availability and consensus of accomplishment: almost every world-famous performing musician visits New York at one time or another during the concert season. This fact does not hold true for any other group of artists. It makes possible the selection of the most outstanding artists in the field and it may also account for a very high consensus in rating creative accomplishment levels—again one of our objective criteria in the selection of artists.

A somewhat related point is the ranking of performers among "great creative artists." In his interview Isaac Stern made a distinction between "interpretive" and "creative" artists, implying that only the latter are the "real creators." Referring specifically to the performing artists interviewed here, the musicologist George Jellinek explains that out of hundreds of excellent musicians with outstanding expertise and technique, only a small percentage become soloists, and of these only an infinitesimal number rank among the greatest performing artists. The difference is the creative spark or genius these few possess. They interpret or recreate written symbols so as to leave their unique imprint.[1] All the artists interviewed here fulfill the conditions for "creativity" as defined by the following criterion: an idea or conception is being expressed in articulate form (literary, musical, visual) and the resulting production has uniqueness as well as excellence. The distinction between *original* creation and *re*creation is an arbitrary one. Even the visual arts predominantly involve imitation or recreation. Despite technical perfection, innumerable paintings and sculptures do not reflect the uniqueness of a great artistic creation. Perhaps the most obvious case in point is modern photography. Whereas some works reflect true artistic creativity, the medium lends itself to a purely

[1]Personal communication. George Jellinek is a music critic and the music director of *The New York Times* radio station, WQXR.

technical representation of the given. Thus, creativity does not depend on the medium in question, but on the way in which that medium is used. Casals once remarked, "The composer is the creator; he creates in black and white. The performer is the recreator—he puts the colors in."

2. With only one exception, all the artists and scientists I interviewed are men. I consider this fact the most severe limitation in the scope of the study. Of nineteen women (artists) contacted by letter, one agreed to the interview, four declined, and fourteen did not reply. Responses to twenty-nine identical letters sent to men resulted in twelve acceptances (but Rubinstein's and Menuhin's did not materialize) five refusals, and twelve unanswered. I did not contact any woman scientists because specific comparisons were to be made between creative artists and creative scientists with sex as one of the variables that had to be kept constant. With the exception of William Shockley, every scientist contacted agreed to be interviewed; however, two scientists later refused to be identified by name. Their interviews are included, labeled "Professor X" and "Professor Y."

I do not know why famous women did not agree to be interviewed. Their refusal puzzles me all the more since I encountered no such resistance in any of the other groups. Of well over 600 people interviewed, half were women. Furthermore, I did not find any sex-related differences in the attitudes toward death in any group.

3. Though I have presented every interview that I conducted with an artist or scientist, I have included only six interviews with people on lower levels of self-actualization. I chose them for various reasons: some because they demonstrated startling differences between truly creative lives and all others; some because they are highly representative of a specific group of people. Such deliberate choices are of necessity biased and impose limits on conclusions drawn on their evidence. However, they are of great heuristic value. If some of the answers from these interviews may be treated with skepticism, the many questions raised by them will, I hope, stimulate further research on the topic. Let me raise just a few of the obvious questions:

(a) Is there, indeed, an overall positive relationship between self-actualization and coming to terms with death? Can one find negative instances such that: (1) The more frustrating life has been, the more positive one's attitude toward death; and (2) the more fulfilling life has been the more negative one's attitude toward death? Both of these positions can certainly be defended on common-sense grounds.

(b) What is the attitude toward death of highly self-actualized individuals who are not truly *creative* or who have not left a mark?

(c) What role does society play in furthering or preventing self-actualization?

(d) Unhappy geniuses exist as well as happy geniuses. The artists and scientists interviewed in this book belong predominantly to the latter kind. Perhaps the former do not grant interviews. Are they likely to have come to terms with death to a greater or a lesser extent?

Some of these and similar questions are raised throughout this book. I hope I have made a beginning in answering a few.

I

The Problem
of Death

1

Fears of Death

It's not the general plan of things
That I should lose my day
I do the work, fulfill myself
And then I'll go away.

—Genia Marburg Reiss

Fear of Death

"I don't think people are afraid of death. What they are afraid of is the incompleteness of their life," wrote Ted Rosenthal (1973), who at the age of thirty was told that he had acute leukemia and was going to die.

This is one of the most positive statements made on the most fundamentally aversive human condition. It contains an implicit solution to the existential fear of death: completion of one's life, attainment of self-fulfillment.

Fear of death is expressed in many forms. When people are asked what it is that they fear about death, the most frequent responses fall roughly into three categories: religiously conditioned fears, separation-abandonment fears, and existential fears. Another fear frequently expressed is of dying painfully. The fear of the process of dying is not identical with the fear of death and will be considered elsewhere.

Religiously conditioned fears involve beliefs in an after-life with prospects of judgment day, hell, purgatory, or rebirth and sometimes are expressed as the fear of the unknown. In these cases the feared condition is not inevitable and can be avoided or at least ameliorated by following some religious doctrines. It rarely engenders the feeling of complete helplessness or panic encountered in other fears of death experiences. Rather, a feeling of having some control over the outcome is pervasive.

Religious fears concern one's precarious relationship with God, whereas separation-abandonment fears center around the sorrow and anguish caused by leaving others behind or by being left behind. The focus here is on interpersonal relationships. Literary works throughout the ages have dealt with human attachment and the despair of discovering that death keeps one rooted to a past that can never be reinstated.

In the year 1400, Von Tepl (1957), The Plowman of Bohemia, wrote his famous argumentative dialogue with Death as a means of coming to terms with the death of his young wife. For centuries the book has served as a consolation for the bereaved. Death personfied argues that the Plowman himself is to blame for his anguish:

> Had you restrained your love, you would be free of sorrow. The greater the love, while one possesses it, the greater the sorrow when one is deprived of it. . . . Unpleasure must follow pleasure . . . [Author's translation]

One is reminded of Francesca's words in Dante's *Inferno*,

> No grief surpasses this . . . in the midst of misery to remember bliss.

Montaigne's essays too are expressions of man's struggle with death. And about 150 years after Von Tepl, Montaigne addressed himself to the same problem. But Montaigne is a Stoic. He has worshiped the Golden Mean and has taken moderate measure to be perfection.

> We must always be ready to go . . . and take special care to have only ourselves to deal with. For we shall have enough trouble without adding any. . . . I can move out when he [God] chooses, without regret for anything at all, unless for life. . . . I unbind myself on all sides; my farewells are already half made to everyone except myself.

He admired the Greek, Stilpo, who, when asked about his losses upon escaping from his burning city—in which he had lost his wife, children, and property—replied, "Thanks to God I have lost nothing of my own." Montaigne concludes that we should have wife, children, goods, and above all, health. But we should not bind ourselves to them so strongly that our happiness depends on them. When the time comes it will be nothing new to us to do without them.

Thus, in the tradition of the Stoics, separation-abandonment fears are not inevitable. We can control them through greater self-centeredness and self-containment.[1] While these fears are rooted to life and its experiences, we do well to remember that the religiously conditioned fears are other-worldly and vague, therefore concerned with a transcendent future. Separation-abandonment, however, catalogues the past.

Montaigne may have come to terms with interpersonal death-related fears, but the existential fear of death still lingers on: "My farewells are already half made to everyone *except myself.*" (Emphasis mine.)

The existential fear of death, the fear of not existing, is the hardest to conquer. Most defensive structures, such as the denial of reality, rationalization, insulation, erected to ward off religiously conditioned and separation-abandonment fears do not lend themselves readily as protective barriers against the existential fear of death. All defense mechanisms are self-deceptive. It is difficult to deceive ourselves about the absolute reality that one day we will cease to exist. The irrevocable finiteness of our existence, which threatens to rob us of all control over our ultimate destiny, is the most unacceptable aspect of the human condition.

Attempts to come to terms with the existential fear of death may take many forms. It may be repressed, externalized, sublimated; one may commit suicide or one may conquer it entirely by experiencing life as completed. Some fight death itself in the belief that they can succeed by abolishing it. Thus, Esfandiary (1974) writes:

> Soon it will be possible to extend human life indefinitely. After thousands of years of desperate struggle against death and deepest anguish at its inevitability there is at last hope of winning that struggle. In research centers around the world efforts are now accelerating to overcome aging and, in time, death itself.

Through the ages, our greatest challenge was to overcome the obstacles and seemingly unconquerable forces in nature; when not able to conquer them entirely, we tried to bend them, change them,

---

[1]Schizophrenic withdrawal is the extreme case of severing relationships with the outside world, as a protection against the intolerable fear of separation: "If I am not a part of the real world, it cannot abandon me."

use them—and finally succeeded at leaving a mark. Perhaps the ultimate goal, the very source of all our endeavors, has always been to
conquer death, though it is a goal that probably cannot and should not
ever be reached. Its attainment would signify the end of all life as we
know and value it. In biology, chemistry, physics, and space explora-
tion, the implicit quest is to understand, to protect, to improve life. The
most obvious examples are the advances made in medicine: the eradi-
ciation of many fatal diseases, the dramatic decrease of infant mortality
and childbirth death, and increased longevity. But far beyond these
most visible conquests, every accomplishment above the animal level
of existence is a direct consequence of the challenge of death. Our very
essence rests on our knowledge of mortality. From the building of
permanent shelters to the invention of means of transportation to ever
more distant places traversed in shorter and shorter time spans, to the
conception and execution of the highest expression in the arts—all this
is founded on our knowledge of death. If there were always tomorrow—if we didn't know that our future was limited—our only goal
would be the satisfaction of immediate, parochial needs, as we witness
it on the animal level.

Perhaps the noblest of human characteristics is our desire to
challenge destiny, and our fight, whatever the odds are, against loss of
control and ultimate extinction. Hugo von Hofmannsthal (1970) closes
his play *The Fool and Death* with Death marveling over our accomplishing the unaccomplishable:

> How wonderful are these creatures who explain the unexplainable, read
> what never has been written, bind the chaotic, and find a pathway in
> eternal darkness. [Author's translation]

Some of the strategies that we engage in seem to be productive
and successful, while others seem unproductive and unsuccessful. I
say "seem to be" because of our subjective and cultural bias in making
these value judgements. Thus, by converting the inevitable event of
death, over which one has no control, into an event of free choice,
suicide may be the most positive means of coming to terms with death
for one individual, while abolishing death entirely may be a catastrophe for all mankind. But there is no doubt that the way we choose to
deal with our fear of death will affect all aspects of our lives.

At the present time, repression is the most common defense

against the existential fear of death. In interviews with close to 700 people from which those in this volume are drawn, the vast majority stated that they "hardly ever" think about their own deaths.

How do we manage to avoid thinking about a highly emotionally charged event that has a 100 percent chance of occurring? For one thing, we try to ban death-related stimuli from our environment. In the last 100 years, from Tolstoy to Kübler-Ross, a great deal has been written on the psychological and physical isolation of those dying in our midst. Nowadays, put in hospitals, they are not only avoided by family and friends, but even neglected by physicians and nurses. We euphemize wakes and funerals, curtail signs of bereavement, neglect the bereaved, and avoid the discussion of our own death with people close to us. We have even managed to avoid introspection that would lead to contemplation of our own death.

Of course, we know that we are mortal and that death is inevitable. But we do not quite believe it. We acknowledge the death of others, but we pay only lip service to our own.

The following interview with a young Indian physicist is a good example of the tricks we play on ourselves. In the first part of the interview I asked K.M. a number of standard interview questions, which he answered freely and with obvious sincerity. He emphasized that he was not afraid of death and that he was only too aware of the fragility of life. He had accepted death long ago as inevitable and was prepared for it at any point in his existence. As a matter of fact, his preference was to die before he got old, since old age would only be a hindrance to his goal in life: to increase understanding through his work. Aside from his need to pursue this goal, he felt unemotional— even cynical—about his death, and he hardly ever thought about it, adding, "certainly not when I am awake, but I occasionally dream about it."

At the end of the interview, which had lasted for about forty minutes, K.M. remarked that it was stimulating to express his thoughts about a subject we so rarely think about. He assured me that the interview had not upset or depressed him in the least, reiterating that he felt emotionally indifferent toward his death. At that point I asked K.M. if he might be willing to explore his feelings on a more concrete level by choosing his preferred time, place, and circumstance of death. He was not sure that he understood, but he was willing to explore it wherever it might take him.

I.: If you had control over it, would you choose to die in the morning, afternoon, evening, or at night?

K.M.: Makes no difference.

I.: Would you prefer to die on a weekend, Saturday or Sunday, or any other particular day of the week?

K.M.: Makes no difference.

I.: Would you prefer to die in spring, summer, fall, or winter?

K.M.: (Interrupting) No preference.

Somewhat irritated, he asked why anyone would consider these questions at all. What difference could the time of death possibly make to anyone? I asked whether he considered his death as an important event in his life. In view of his earlier assurances of emotional indifference toward his death, his reply was somewhat surprising:

K.M.: Yes, probably one of the most important events.

I.: Are you absolutely certain that it will occur at a specific time and season?

K.M.: Yes.

I.: What about other important events in your future, which are less certain to occur? Do you have a preference as to the time of a trip, even whether to take a night or a day flight? The time of a meeting with someone important? The time and season of your wedding or of any other celebration?

He reluctantly agreed that he had indeed time preferences for most anticipated events.

I.: If you could choose the location of your death, such as indoors, outdoors, in bed, on a meadow, in water—

K.M.: (interrupting) Not in water! [He did not elaborate or make any choice of a preferred place.]

I.: Would you rather be alone at the moment of your death or have one or more persons present?

K.M.: Alone.

I.: Would you prefer not to know about time, place, and circumstances of your death?

K.M.: (emphatically) Yes, I don't want to know!

I.: You said earlier that you hardly ever think about your own death. Which one of the following statements applies best to your feelings:
I *avoid* thinking about my own death.
I find it unpleasant to think about my death.
I like full awareness of my death.

He ignored the first statement; interrupted the second with "Very!" "Extremely!" and said "No" to the third.

K.M.'s mood had changed drastically. He had become less verbal, his former enthusiasm had vanished, and he said that the questions had depressed him. We explored the reasons for the change that had taken place. K.M. felt that he had been forced to acknowledge the impact of his mortality. He could no longer treat death as something abstract, that occurred at "another" time, at "another" place, under "different" or vague circumstances.

K.M.: I suddenly *knew* that the day of my death will be on a Monday, Tuesday, Wednesday, Thursday, Friday, Saturday, or Sunday; on one single, specific day. When I said "makes no difference" I meant that I didn't like any of the possible choices.

He now doubted his earlier statement of accepting death at any point in his existence. He had been fairly successful at repressing the idea of his own death. However, as is typical in repression, it had manifested itself in his dreams.

One may wonder where the advantage lies in confronting one's own death, since it cannot be prevented anyway, and since it leads to an increase in anxiety. Montaigne (1965) weighed the alternatives of "ridding ourselves of the thought of death" or of "having nothing on our minds as often as death." At first he argues for the former alternative: "I passed the age of 39 years, and I need at least that many more; but to be bothered meanwhile by the thought of a thing so far off would be folly." In the same vein he states:

Nothing can be so grievous that happens only once. Is it reasonable so long to fear a thing so short?

It [death] does not concern you dead or alive; alive, because you are; dead, because you are no more.

What does it matter, you will tell me, how it happens, provided we do not worry about it? I am of that opinion; and in whatever way we can put ourselves in shelter from blows, even under a calf's skin, I am not the man to shrink from it.

He agrees with Horace:

If but my faults could trick and please my wits,
I'd rather seem a fool at ease, than be wise and rage.

But he comes to the conclusion that we cannot fool ourselves:

But it is folly to expect to get there that way. . . . They go, they come, they trot, they dance—of death no news. . . . But when it comes, either to them or their wives, children or friends, surprising them unprepared and defenseless what torments . . . what despair overwhelms them! . . . We must provide for this earlier. . . . Let us learn to meet it steadfastly and to combat it. . . . Let us rid it of its strangeness, come to know it; get used to it.

What is gained by this brave confrontation? According to Montaigne:

Premeditation of death is premeditation of freedom. He who has learned how to die has unlearned how to be a slave. Knowing how to die frees us from all subjection and constraint. . . . He who would teach men to die would teach them to live.

The attempt to ban death from our consciousness is not only unsuccessful, but also detrimental to the quality of our lives. Even if we succeed in repressing the content of our fears, the feelings attached to it will manifest themselves in the form of vague, free-floating anxiety. We can never get rid of the fear unless we know what it is that we are fearing. Since repression is never fully successful, it is an ongoing process, demanding constant investment of energy, energy that might otherwise be channeled into more productive accomplishments.

Coming to Terms with Death

Artistic creations are the prime example of the product of such sublimated energy. This does not mean that creative people do not fear death. But it does mean that they deal with it in a different manner.

Freud ascribed all cultural achievements to the mechanism of sublimation, the channeling of energy into socially desirable forms.

In a strictly psychoanalytic sense, however, sublimation still implies repression of the anxiety-arousing thought or instinct (death, aggression, sex), which can manifest itself only in disguised form. An added dimension to the process of sublimation is best described by the term *externalization*. In externalization, as used here, the creative product is a representation or imitation of the anxiety-arousing thought or feeling itself. And, indeed, the death theme runs through all forms of artistic creation.

A recurring observation in the literature on art is that the greatest works are the product of the artist's struggle to find meaning in the human condition, in the struggle of coming to terms with the reality of death (Alvarez, 1970; Lamont, 1973; Nelson, 1973).

In a discussion of the Romantic artists who could express and purge their inward tragedy in an art form, Alvarez (1970), made the following remark about Nerval's suicide: "He was one of the very few writers who finally acted out the Romantic agony to its logical end. The rest contented themselves with writing about it." In other words, they externalized their inner conflicts.

After interviewing creative artists and scientists, Rosner and Abt (1970) concluded that literary creations are generally autobiographical in one way or another and, in that sense, self-expression is seen most directly. I would add that all creative products are autobiographical in the sense that they are projections of the artist's innermost feelings. Expression of these innermost feelings is the very content of art. And death holds center stage. Artists write about death, represent death in paintings, symbolize or interpret it in music and dance.

To interpret or symbolize death requires actively dealing with the reality of death. By transforming death into a product of our own creation, we gain some control over it. It is a way of doing actively what otherwise we must suffer passively. But such recreation or imitation demands an intimate relationship with death. This intimacy arises through introspection or internalization. In the latter, death is an integral part of one's existence. It is a constant presence of which one may or may not be fully aware, while introspection is an entirely conscious process, leading to full acknowledgment of the reality of death. Full acknowledgment of one's finiteness is a crucial step in conquering the existential fear of death.

Thus, Feifel (1959) remarked that in gaining awareness of death we sharpen and intensify our awareness of life. He describes the knowledge of one's finiteness as a galvanizing force, a *vis à tergo*, pushing man forward toward creativity and accomplishment.

Kaufmann (1976) developed the thesis that once one accepts the fact that one must die, of the limited amount of time at one's disposal, death becomes a powerful incentive:

> The man who accepts his death may find in this experience a strong spur to making something of his life and may succeed in some accomplishment that robs him of the fear of death.

Once one has succeeded in giving form and structure to the possibilities within oneself, once one's unique potentials have been actualized, " . . . the picture changes: I have won the race and in a sense have triumphed over death. Death comes too late" (Kaufmann, 1976).

Ted Rosenthal's statement should be recalled: "I don't think people are afraid of death. What they are afraid of is the incompleteness of their life."

Thus, the existential fear of death can be conquered by reaching self-fulfillment and, as a consequence, experiencing life as completed. The startling differences in attitudes toward death between people of varying stages of self-fulfillment will be explored in the succeeding chapters.

2

Timely and Untimely Death

For us leading physicists, the distinction between past, present and future is only an illusionary one.

—*Albert Einstein*

Natural Death

In today's vernacular, a death is termed "natural" unless it is caused by accident, suicide, or medical neglect. Natural death connotes a more appropriate or timely end than nonnatural death.

Yet this differentiation is superficial: while it takes into account physical functions, it wholly ignores psychological ones. Despite the twentieth century's emphasis on the psychosoma, the popular tendency is to identify an "appropriate" death solely with the exhaustion of physical potentiality. The old cliché "the mind is willing but the flesh is weak" has been accepted as an unalterable truism. Thus, we accept a death as natural when physical functions fail, regardless of the individual's state of mental fulfillment at the final hour.

The longevity potential of most organisms has been fairly accurately established and is consistent with the full development of innate structures and functions. The human longevity potential has been estimated at 137 to 150 years. Although man's life span has more than doubled within the last century, it is still only at about half its potential duration. As a consequence, our attitude toward death is paradoxical: on one hand, we accept death as "natural" since it usually occurs as the result of an expected failure of physical functions. On the other hand, we think of death as an outside force which "unjustly" abridges life processes. In the latter view, death is anything but a natural part of our existence; it is an event which never awaits our chosen moment of "completion," of utter self-fulfillment. This suggests that the death of a man or woman today is *almost always* premature.

In light of a systematic synchronicity we encounter at all levels of the animal kingdom, it is strange indeed that this dramatic human life-span differential between the physical and mental functions is so rarely questioned.

Rudolf Ehrenberg (1923; 1925), the biologist, formulated a principle which states that the formation of structures is the essence of life. Once all unstructured potential is converted into structure, death occurs, since any further life processes are impossible. At the moment of total structurization, life has completed itself. Montaigne must have understood the principle of structurization long before it was formulated. Some 350 years before Ehrenberg he wrote:

> All the time you live you steal from life; living is at life's expense. The constant work of your life is to build death.

And Jung's concepts of individuation and the transcendent function are the psychological counterparts of Ehrenberg's biological principle. For Jung, the ultimate aim of life is the full differentiation, development, and, finally, integration of each system and function of personality. When all potentials are actualized and integrated—this is the equivalent of full structurization—one has reached wholeness, completeness, self-realization. But Jung is aware that this goal is an ideal, in fact never attained by a living organism. He explains the necessity for death at the point of completion in physical terms: when all systems are fully developed they are in a state of perfect balance. This is a tensionless state. But energy can be produced only when systems are in imbalance. Without the generation of energy a system runs down and stops. He refers to this state as entropy, which is incompatible with life (Jung, 1960).

Ehrenberg and Jung arrive at the same conclusion: when all potentials in an individual are actualized, life is no longer possible. Life is completed. It is at *this* point that death can be regarded as "natural."

Literally speaking, "completion" signals to us that an event has "come to an end." But the dictionary also defines "completion" as "perfect," "entire," or "fulfilled." When an event has reached the stage of completion, there is nothing more to be hoped for or feared with regard to it. Thus, the consequences of experiencing life as completed should be dramatic; seen from this vantage point, we might expect death to be a goal one strives for rather than a threat. Here, the human condition would no longer seem absurd; life and death would no longer be devoid of all meaning. Death *as the completion of life* could rightly be called a "natural" death.

But can we ever actualize all of our potential?

Physical and Mental Longevity

The first problem that presents itself is the discrepancy between our physical and mental conditions. In the vast majority of contemporary deaths, physical functions fail long before mental ones do. This condition alone forecloses any possibility of fully actualizing our psychological potentials.

We do not have any scientific evidence which shows that physical and mental longevity potentials are equivalent. However, as pointed out above, the assumption of a congruency between them is in keeping with all other longevity patterns found in any given species. No organ (whether we consider the liver, the kidney, the heart, or the eye) is known to have a shorter or longer longevity potential than any other. However, when one organ fails it often affects all others. If the life-span potential of all human functions is, in fact, equivalent, then the current assumption of an overabundance of psychological potential that can never be actualized is incorrect. The problem lies rather in the premature failure of physical processes. If today's average human life span were extended to full capacity—that is, to 150 years—it might very well be brought into line with man's psychological potentials. And with the scientific advances we have witnessed in the last few decades, there is little doubt that we are *capable* of dramatically increasing longevity in the not too distant future—just as we are capable of foreshortening or altogether destroying life on earth. Which way we go all depends on the political, scientific, and sociological options we will choose.

The fear of dying prematurely—that is, before one's psychological needs have been satisfied—was voiced over and over again in the interviews I conducted. Statements such as these were common: "I am afraid of dying before I have done 'my thing,' " ". . . there is still so much I want to do," "I haven't really lived," "I want to be able to finish

my work." Perhaps the most eloquent expression of the fear of premature death is contained in Keats' sonnet:

> When I have fears that I may cease to be
> Before my pen has gleaned my teeming brain . . .

Once our physical survival is commensurate with the actualization of
our psychological potentials, our orientation toward life and attitude
toward death are bound to change.

But longevity is not the only problem. It may not even be the most
important one. Self-actualization requires more than a long life; objective duration, as measured by minutes, months, or millenia, comprises
only one aspect of a person's time perspective.

There are innumerable examples of geniuses (Mozart, Schubert,
Shelley, Byron, Keats) who reached extraordinary levels of self-
actualization, although they died in their thirties. Conversely, millions
of people reach old age without ever actualizing a small fraction of their
potentials. Montaigne wrote:

> The advantage of living is not measured by length but by use; some men
> have lived long and lived little; attend to it while you are in it. It lies in
> your will, not in the number of years . . .

Very much the same thought is conveyed by Ted Rosenthal:

> . . . You can live a lifetime in a day; you can live a lifetime in a moment;
> you can live a lifetime in a year . . .

What makes some people capable of cramming a lifetime into a
year while others have "lived little" no matter how long they have
lived? Again, the difference lies, at least in part, in how keenly one is
aware of the limited amount of time at one's disposal.

Awareness of Finiteness

A pervasive human characteristic is to value most what one cannot
have or whatever is in short supply. An unfortunate result is that we
appreciate life most fully when we are about to lose it—often, when it

is too late to make use of it. Only a few are aware of their impending death throughout life, as Montaigne was. This universal human tragedy is the theme of Hofmannsthal's play, *The Fool and Death.* Claudio, suddenly confronted by Death, tries to convince him that his time for dying has not yet come:

> Remember, before the leaf glides to the ground,
> It has drained all its sap:
> I am far from that point: I have not lived!
> . . . my young days have slipped away,
> And I never knew that even this meant life.
> . . . Half hearted, my senses numb,
> In every consummation mysteriously inhibited,
> Never feeling my inner self aglow,
> Nor ever swept away by mighty waves;
> Never upon my path met God,
> With whom one strives, until He grants His blessing.

When Death argues that Claudio should have been able "to animate this chaos of dead things with relatedness, to make your garden out of it," Claudio still protests.

> I shall cling to this clod of earth,
> The deepest longing for life cries out in me.
> Now I feel—oh, let me—that I can live!

After his life is passed in review, Claudio asks,

> Why did this happen to me? Why, Death,
> Must you be the one to teach me to see life . . .

At the end, Claudio resolves his conflict:

> Since my life was death, then Death be my life! . . .
> You can pour more life into one hour,
> Than my whole life contained . . .
> Never, with all my living senses
> Have I perceived so much, and so I call it good!
> . . . For only as I die, I feel that I am.   *[Author's translation]*

One is reminded of Jesse Stuart's (1956) line: "No man really begins to live until he has come close to dying." Similarly, Avery Weisman (1972) wrote, "Human values seem to be enhanced when we become aware that death always surrounds us, like the shadow that illuminates the substance." This statement is dramatically illustrated by the following encounter.

At a conference on death and dying a few years ago, a thirty-two-year-old man, terminally ill with leukemia, was one of the speakers. He had been on a lecture tour for several months, trying to get a difficult message across to his audiences. He was harsh and visibly angry with us—not because he was dying, but because he felt that we were not "living." He told us that we looked at him and thought "this young man is dying," while we ignored the fact that we *too* were dying. He told us that he was the only one around who was truly alive, aware of the preciousness of each moment.

At this point I asked him whether he wouldn't be willing to change places with any one of us. "Yes," he responded, "but only if I could keep this perspective, this quality of being alive; not if I were just to continue living 'half-dead,' as most of you do. I am afraid this is an orientation one gains only when one knows that one's days are numbered. I guess we can't have it both ways."

Why can't we have it both ways? Why must we wait until we are touched by death to reel around and begin to live our lives? Why can't we advantageously structure our time perspective at the beginning of life, when there is still time to actualize our ideas, talents, and dreams, rather than at the end, when most of our life lies in the past?

The time perspective of those condemned to death is unique: terminally ill patients or inhabitants of death row know that death will occur within a specific, relatively narrow time span. On the other hand, we "the living" can *pretend* that we are not condemned to death; after all, we have no idea when we are going to die. Death can be kept at arm's length, can be thought of as a vague, far-off phenomenon just as long as the time of its occurrence is uncertain. But this also requires an ill-defined, amorphous future orientation.

This line of thought leads us to the following conclusions: (1) To live life to the fullest demands a full acknowledgment of one's own death. (2) Our attitude toward death is inextricably intertwined with our time perspective. And as long as we deny our mortality, we cannot move into the future. "If death frightens us, how is it possible to go a step forward without feverishness?" asks Montaigne.

Time Perspective

Man is confined to three time dimensions: past, present, and future. Some aspects of these dimensions are seemingly absolute, objective facts commonly shared by all men. Others are relative and changeable and depend on subjective experiences. Thus, objectively, we think of time as a linear, orderly sequence, moving from the past through the present into the future. But subjectively, time may be experienced as "always now" or "never now"; some live primarily in the past, others in the future.

While most of us feel confident that we can objectively "keep track" of time with clocks and calendars, where did time go when an event experienced years ago seems to have occurred "just yesterday"? How is it that a minute is sometimes suspended, as if lasting for hours? In our experiences, time may be fleeing, dragging, standing still, or even going backwards. Objective time has no strongly defined beginning or end, but our own horizons may be narrow or broad. Thus, some individuals have constricted time perspectives, venturing no further than into the immediate past or the immediate future. Others have perspectives which encompass vast temporal regions.

Recognizing this double nature of time, Weisman (1972) distinguishes the chronological from the existential. Chronological time is public property: it depends on a public consensus. Weisman points to the impingement of existential time on chronological time. But equally important is the influence chronological time has on our subjective experience of time. Public consensus is not based on inviolable laws of nature, but on cultural indoctrination. A few examples will demonstrate our culturally determined bias for a past rather than a future orientation, a bias which wields far-reaching influence on our subjective experience of time.

Age is measured universally by way of an individual's past trajectory, rather than by an assessment of future potentials.[1] On the basis of "how many years someone has been around since birth," we are tagged with a number, a figure which has come to represent far more than what we are actually measuring. This number, which fits some well and some ill, is the sole criterion for classifying individuals as "young," "middle-aged," or "old." Accordingly, we prejudge what they are capable of and what we can expect from them as well as from ourselves. And true to the self-fulfilling prophecy, we live up to our expectations. Only a few are capable of transcending this "objective" age assessment. Thus, when questioned about his experience of time, Isaac Stern remarked:

> It is relative. I look at my "old" friend, X, who is in his sixties and at my "young" friend, Arthur Rubinstein, who is ninety years old. Time is relative. It can't be measured in years. It depends on the person. Everybody is different.

Assessing an individual's capacity—physical, mental, or psychological—from a past perspective has an insidious effect on the medical profession as well. I have repeatedly heard physicians remark, "What can you expect of someone his age?" or "For her age she is doing fine." Often doctors imply by this that corrective measures fit for a younger person are not worthwhile attempting for an older one. The individual potential is largely ignored in favor of generalized norms.

A second example, taken from clinical psychology, illustrates the role of cultural indoctrination even more convincingly. Freud has been criticized for focusing his developmental orientation entirely on a person's past in assessing personality and, more specifically, neurotic conflicts. Because of his emphasis on the past and his postulation of the repetition compulsion (the tendency to relive past experiences), Freud has been characterized as pessimistic. In contrast, the "self-actualization" theorists take into account a person's strivings, ambitions, hopes, and goals and are regarded as more optimistic. But Freud's assessment is, unfortunately, the more realistic outlook and will remain so until we effect dramatic changes in our cultural indoctrination.

[1]In his *Theoretical Biology*, Ehrenberg (1923) measures the age of an organism by its yet-to-be actualized potentials, that is, from death to the present, rather than from birth to the present. This alternate form of assessing age will be discussed in chapter 10.

One of the prevalent symptoms in neurosis, as well as in psychosis, is guilt. This guilt stems from commissions or omissions in our past. But in ten years of clinical practice, I have not once encountered a patient who felt guilty regarding *the future*. That is, guilty about something s/he "ought" to do in the future but knows that s/he will not or cannot do. The fact that guilt feelings are rooted in the past stems from cultural indoctrination. Clinical studies have invariably shown that feelings of guilt develop in childhood and are based on prevailing cultural values as transmitted by our parents. In different cultures the content of such feeling varies or may even be absent. When children are made to feel guilty it is usually for something they have done, rather than for something they will not do in the future. Yet there is no rational explanation why possible future omissions should or could not be stressed as much as past mistakes. As a matter of fact, we have greater control and freedom over future events than over past ones. Guilt feelings about past events are gratuitous. We cannot undo them. Freedom of choice and responsibility dwell in the future. We can make plans and effect changes only for that part of our lives which we have not yet lived. Kastenbaum and Aisenberg (1972) have labeled the past "used time," in which things can never rehappen or unhappen. The past is history—constituted of given facts and, at times, of mismanaged memory—while we constitute the future out of possibilities.

The felicity of a shift from a past orientation to a future one has been echoed innumerable times. Thus, Victor Frankl (1971) wrote:

> It is a peculiarity of man that he can only live by looking to the future—
> *sub specie aeternitatis*. . . . A man who let himself decline because he could
> not see any future goal found himself occupied with retrospective
> thoughts. . . . They preferred to close their eyes and to live in the past.
> Life for such people became meaningless.

Most recently, Maddi (1978) described personality as a blend of facticity and possibility. The former are givens of biological, social, and present states that stem from decisions made in the past; the latter is the pursuit of future states. One may choose either as a predominating factor in orienting one's life. Choosing the past jeopardizes growth and engenders ontological guilt, experienced as missed opportunities. If the past is chosen regularly, guilt accumulates into despair and meaninglessness. One's life is then perceived as having been wasted.

Choosing the future is regarded as superior, because it is the way of growth, development, vitality, and renewal. But the future also has its dangers and risks, since we have only partial control over it. Thus, pursuing possibility brings ontological anxiety or fear of the unknown (Maddi, 1978).

It looks as if we are damned if we do and damned if we do not, assuming that the choice is, indeed, between feeling guilty and feeling anxious. However, I do not think we really have this choice. Those who fear the unknown do not "choose" the future. They are stuck in the past. It has the reassuring attribute of familiarity. We are "accustomed" to our past; we own it. There is also comfort in its immutability. It does not make any demands of us; rather, it frees us of our responsibility to effect changes. Those who live in the past do not feel pressured into activity. Feelings frequently associated with a past orientation are acceptance, resignation, regret, and guilt. No matter how miserable it may have been, one hardly ever feels terror about one's own past. The future, on the other hand, is often dreaded. Because it is unknown, anything can happen at any moment. Most importantly, death will invariably happen in the future.

Kastenbaum and Aisenberg (1972) have pointed out that apprehension about death may be one of the main factors in the tendency by some to rein in thoughts of futurity, impairing their ability to plan ahead, to anticipate both hazards and opportunities. They also found that young people with low death anxiety show significantly greater extension into the future, while those with high death concern show a more limited tendency to project or plan. But we can actualize our potentials only in the future, not in the past. Thus, if fear of death inhibits our ability to plan, it also restricts all movement toward accomplishment and self-fulfillment.

Recent life-review studies of old or terminally ill patients show that if a person looks on the past in despair, feeling that life has been wasted, s/he cannot come to terms with death (Butler, 1963). Herman Feifel (1965) has observed that the human crisis is primarily one of the "waste of limited years, the unassayed tasks, the locked opportunities, the talents withering in disuse." On the one hand, these unresolved conflicts keep an individual tied to the past and make him incapable of "letting go." On the other hand, fear of death blocks all movement into the future, where death is waiting.

Clearly, self-actualization demands a future rather than a past orientation. But shouldn't we expect that the very people who had a "good past" would want to hang on to it, while those with unhappy memories would try to forget them? We found just the opposite to be true. Those who experienced the past as unhappy reported most frequently that they were nostalgic, lived mostly in the past, and most surprisingly, even wished they could bring it back—on occasion, to have a chance to do things differently.

The self-actualized individuals, however, showed complete disinterest in the past. If specifically questioned about the quality of their past lives, they would recall the positive aspects in remarks such as: "I had a good life," "I enjoyed every moment of it," "It is thanks to my past that I am who and where I am now." But they never daydream about it. We may get the flavor of their time orientation best by citing some of the typical responses to the question, "In your experience of time, which dimension seems to be the most important one—past, present, or future?"

Eugene P. Wigner, 1963 Nobel Prize recipient in physics:

> I am future-oriented—and present, to a point. . . . I am already looking forward to seeing something very exciting going on on the floor below [some scientific breakthrough]. . . . Even now, though I am interested in your questions, I am mostly oriented to the future. But the past, not at all. I even forget events in the past. I am least interested in it.

Nathan Milstein, violinist:

> Certainly not the past! The past is so unimportant to me, I am not even interested in history. Present and future [are important]. Living is important.

Ronald L. Graham, mathematician:

> . . . remember the better things of the past and enjoy them in the present. I enjoy and participate actively in the present. But in a way you always live right in the future. In order to bring about the future you want, you must plan for it now.

Why this lack of interest in the past in these highly self-actualized individuals? Primarily for the very same reasons which make the past such a safe haven for those who cannot move toward the future. The past comprises only givens; it holds no surprises. The challenges, the excitement, and the opportunities are in the future—with its risks and possibilities.

The Ultimate Goal

We are now in a position to review the major concepts developed thus far:

1. Fear of death is primarily fear of dying prematurely, before we have actualized our potentials.
2. Full acknowledgment of our finiteness intensifies our awareness of life—of the limited amount of time at our disposal—and acts as a galvanizing force, propelling us toward the realization of our talents or desires.
3. If we succeed in giving form to the unique possibilities within ourselves we experience self-fulfillment. At this point, life is completed and death can truly be called a natural one.

But the view of death as the ultimate goal reached at the completion of all life-processes may be an "ideal" one. As long as one is alive, life may always be experienced as incomplete by the restless, active mind. We may forever strive for something just beyond the accomplished, reflecting the human need to transcend the given. Browning's Andrea del Sarto mused, "Ah, but a man's reach should exceed his grasp, or what is a heaven for." Whether total self-actualization has ever been attained, we may never know for certain. But the experience of self-fulfillment may not lie in actually reaching the ultimate goal, but in the satisfaction and success of the hunt—of striving toward that goal. There are certainly quantitative and qualitative differences in self-actualization and in self-fulfillment. There are also different degrees to which one can come to terms with death.

Following Ehrenberg's (1923) principle of structurization and Kaufmann's (1976) position on conquering the fear of death through self-actualization, we assume that the more one has actualized one's potentials, the less one should fear death; the less the level of self-actualization, the greater one's fear of death.[2] This assumption is independent of chronological age.[3]

[2]"Fear of death" is used here as a summary term for all the negative feelings that must be dealt with if one is to come to terms with death. Though fear is perhaps the most frequent and the most aversive aspect that needs to be conquered, it is not the only one. Regret, anger, dislike at having to die may be experienced rather than fear.

[3]Chronological age per se does not account for a critical increase or decrease in fear of death, although age is likely to be related to the degree to which one has fulfilled one's potentials. The failure of keeping levels of self-actualization constant probably accounts for much of the contradictory findings on this issue (reviewed by Kastenbaum & Aisenberg, 1972).

Such levels can, to a large degree, be objectively assessed by creative accomplishments because self-fulfillment, although a subjective experience, increases with goal accomplishment. Put in the simplest form, the more one has done one's "own thing" the more one feels satisfied with life—and, by implication, can better deal with the prospect of death.

II
The
Interviews

3

Introduction to the Interview Process

Introduction to the Interviews

The interviews presented here are those I personally conducted with highly self-actualized people. They will be contrasted with those assessed as medium and as low on the scale of self-actualization.[1] We are primarily concerned with the qualitative differences in their experience of life and in their attitudes toward death. Relative fear of death was assessed on an overall clinical evaluation of the interviews and on phenomenal, that is, subjectively experienced, time perspectives.

The interviews ranged from thirty minutes to two hours, depending on the eagerness of the participant to engage in a free exchange of ideas and feelings.

The interviews reported here fell into a sequence of three stages:

1. A conversation stage which centered primarily around one of two topics—their work or thoughts and feelings about death.
2. A standard interview schedule consisting of ten to fifteen direct and open-ended questions followed by the respondents' ratings of the meaning of the concept of "life" and the concept of "death" along a seven-point (semantic differential) scale.
3. A conversation stage which invariably dealt with the respondents' feelings about death. The first and the third stage, as well as the rating scale, were at times omitted.

[1]The criteria for classification are discussed in the Introduction. Table 3-1 contains the description and classification of the interviewees.

Table 3–1

Description of Ten Groups on the Basis of Age and Self-actualization

Group	Self-actualization Level	Number	Description	Age Range	Mean Age
Young Adults (17–34 yrs.)					
1	High	24	Ivy League College students	17–24	21
2	Medium	46	College students	17–26	21
3	Low	31	Social drop-outs, un-employed	18–34	24
Mature (37–72 yrs.)					
4	High	20	Creative artists and scientists	37–72	54
5	Medium	30	Professionals	37–72	53
6	Low	20	No occupational pre-ference (social drop-outs)	36–73	55
Control					
7		40		21–27	24
8	Random	40	Random	28–38	33
9		40		39–48	43
10		40		50–79	58

Most of the interviews were not recorded. I took notes during and immediately following the interviews. Only responses to the Standard Interview questions are given verbatim. Discussions during the first and third stages are reported only if they shed some light on the respondent's personality or attitude toward death or if they are of special interest in view of the prominence of the participant. The transcribed interviews as they appear in the following pages were sent to those interviewed for deletions and additions, if necessary, and for approval to be published.

The Standard Interview Schedule

The first set of open-ended questions was intended to tap the respondents' goal-directedness and level of self-fulfillment (Goodman, 1975). Though the wording varied somewhat, they were generally formulated in the following terms:

> What do you *really* want out of life?
> What do you consider your highest or ultimate goal?
> What do you consider as the height of fulfillment?
> Have you reached it?
> Do you think you will reach it?

Whenever the respondent had difficulty in deciding on or expressing long-range goals, two broad categories were suggested: (1) The goal of accomplishment, such as increasing understanding, creating, discovering, and finding meaning; (2) More tangible or material goals such as fame, recognition, wealth, and power.

The importance of a given goal and their own commitment to it was assessed by the investment they were ready to make: "How far would you be willing to go, or to sacrifice, to achieve your goal?" If suggestions were necessary, it was pointed out that for some people immediate satisfaction remains so important that no sacrifice would be considered for future goals, while other people might willingly endure hardships or abstinence from any activity or even die for their goal or cause, as in the case of explorers, inventors, and martyrs.

Answers to these questions provided the subjective criteria of experienced or anticipated levels of self-fulfillment. They also differentiated those intrinsically motivated from extrinsically motivated individuals.

The next set of questions concern phenomenological time perspectives on the conscious and fantasy levels. The respondents were asked whether they focused primarily on the past, present, or future and whether they were aware of the limited amount of time they had available to them. If they could not determine their dominant time orientation, they were presented with a series of statements, which they evaluated as applicable or nonapplicable to their own experiences. Examples of these statements:

"I am living mostly in the past."
"I wish I could bring back the past."
"The past is only important as it affects the present (or future)."
"I wish I could hold on to (prolong) every present moment."
"I am eagerly anticipating (planning for) the future."
"I am indifferent to the future."
"I am overwhelmingly aware of time passing, of the limited amount of time available."

After considering these options, people were able to determine their own dominant time orientation.

We have previously discussed how time and death concepts are irradicably intertwined, and why people with a relatively high fear of death are expected to be predominantly past oriented, while those less fearful of death will manifest a predominantly future orientation. The differences between individuals ranking high or low on the self-actualization dimension were dramatic.[2] The group of highly creative people was predominantly future oriented while those at the lowest end of the spectrum were primarily past oriented (Goodman, 1976).

Another facet of a person's subjective time dimension and perhaps an even more critical indicator of one's attitude toward death is the breadth of the phenomenal time perspective. Previous research has indicated that fear of death constricts one's time perspective (Kastenbaum, 1959; Seiden, 1969; Spilka, 1970), which results in focusing on the safest, most familiar time region: the present, the immediate past, and the immediate future. Those least apprehensive of death are free to explore vaster, unfamiliar time regions and can therefore project their needs, wishes, thoughts, and, when applicable, their own person into the far distant future as well as extend themselves into the far distant past. The breadth of this forward and backward extension into time was assessed on a fantasy level by two questions:

1. "Imagine that after death you could come back once, for a short period of time. When would you choose to come back: 2 years, 10 years, 100 years, or 1,000 years after you died?"
2. "If you could visit a period in the past, before you were born,

[2] Only some of the highlights are reported here, since we are primarily interested in the individual cases. Therefore the interviews with each artist and scientist are rendered in full in chapters 4 and 6.

which period would you choose: two to ten years before your birth, around 1900, 1700 to 1900, antiquity, or any other period?"

Both of these questions had the advantage of taking the respondent by surprise; they were extremely fruitful in triggering off death-related feelings *not* tapped by direct questions. Since there are no "right" or "wrong" answers, all of the choices seemed equally "socially acceptable." The responses, especially to the first question, were the most discriminating ones, with self-actualization being negatively related to the two to ten year interval and positively related to the 100 and 1,000 year intervals. The least self-actualized overwhelmingly selected the former category, while the artists and scientists preferred the latter, vaster time span (Goodman, 1976).

The consistency between expectation and preference regarding longevity was determined by responses to the questions: "How long do you *expect* to live?" and "Regardless of your expectations, what is your *preference* regarding time of death?" (from Kastenbaum, 1977). Answers to these questions are clearly multidetermined with neither age nor level of self-actualization a major factor.

Conscious fear of death was assessed by responses to the question, "Are you afraid of death?" An affirmative answer can usually be taken at face value since it would be highly unlikely for individuals to say that they are afraid of it if they harbor no such fear. However, negative responses remain more difficult to assess since fear is frequently denied or repressed with a fair amount of success. An absence of "thinking about" death is often mistaken for an absence of fear. At times a simple pretense is made because in our culture such fears are socially unacceptable and regarded as "unmanly." Thus, the immediate reaction is frequently, "No, I am not afraid!" Follow-up questions usually reveal ambivalence, fear, or genuine success at dealing with the prospect of one's own death.

The last question deals with preoccupation with death: "How often do you think about your own death? Daily, approximately once a week, about once a month, hardly ever?" (Dickstein, 1966). Since full acknowledgment of one's finiteness is presumably a necessary step in the quest of coming to terms with death, one may expect a negative relationship between the frequency of thinking about death and fear of death. However, we found no relationship between fear and the frequency of thinking about it. The most frequently occurring choice in all groups is "hardly ever."

Death and Life Rating Scales (Semantic Differentials)

Do people have an overall positive or negative attitude toward death? If so, is it in any way related to levels of fulfillment? Is there a relationship between one's attitude toward death and one's attitude toward life? To obtain an overall indicator of attitudes toward life and death, a seven-point scale was devised consisting of eight oppositional adjectives along which the respondents rated their feelings of the two concepts (Goodman, 1975). The adjectives (identical for both "Life" and "Death") were:

> cruel—kind
> solitary—united
> desperate—joyful
> unfair—fair
> violent—gentle
> dull—stimulating
> chaotic—harmonious
> worthless—valuable

The respondents inidicated the degree to which they considered these attributes to correspond to their view of death and life by placing a mark on the seven-point scale from a –3 to a +3 including neutral. Without going into detailed statistical analysis, we can answer some of the questions that puzzled us: the vast majority of people have an overall negative attitude toward death and a positive attitude toward life. However, the artists as a group rated death positively while scientists rated death slightly negatively; those with lowest fulfillment rated death most negatively and life most negatively. Artists and scientists both rated life quite positively.

We found that the more positively one evaluates life, the more positively one tends to evaluate death; the less positively one views life, the more negatively one views death. On rare occasions death was rated highly positively while life was rated as highly negative. In these cases follow-up interviews revealed suicidal tendencies. In most cases suicide attempts had already been made and in one case suicide was committed about six months after the interview. Thus, the rating scale may be a valuable measure in assessing suicide risks.

Interestingly, scientists and artists differ considerably in the qualities they attribute to death. For example, none of the artists views death as cruel, but half of the scientists do. On the other hand, most artists thought of death as stimulating while none of the scientists did. Scientists are also more likely to view death as chaotic while most artists rated it as harmonious.

On the basis of our interviews we can conclude that the relationship between levels of self-actualization and fear of death indicators is indeed a negative one with the most significant differences occurring between highly creative individuals and those most paralyzed in pursuing self-fulfilling activities.

The Age Factor

The relationship of age to fear of death is rather complex. When the self-actualization dimension is kept constant, the fear of death indicators increase with age. However, when levels of self-fulfillment are introduced, age plays only a minor role; indeed, the above-mentioned relationship is at times reversed. Thus, older people who have reached a high level of fulfillment fear death less than young people, although the latter might be highly actualized themselves. But older people who do not feel they have realized their goals fear death more than younger people. Age must certainly play a role in terms of regrets and decreased hope to be able to make up for lost opportunities. Young people are protected by a buffer zone—time. They can deceive themselves rather easily into believing that they will do "their thing" tomorrow—that they still have time to make up for "lost time." Older people, however, are more likely to sense that it is too late, that life has passed them by and that they have missed their opportunities. Indeed, these were the recurring statements made by people who felt they had no more time to actualize their potentials.

I stated initially that people are not afraid of death itself, but of the incompleteness of life, of dying prematurely. If by "dying prematurely" we meant chronological prematurity, then older people would be less afraid of death than younger people. But our findings clearly contradict this: premature death is not determined by longevity but by the actualization of an individual's potential.

4

Interviews with Artists

"A single summer grant me, great powers, and
A single autumn for fully ripened song
That, sated with the sweetness of my
Playing, my heart may more willingly die.

The soul that, living, did not attain its divine
Right cannot repose in the nether world.
But once what I am bent on, what is
Holy, my poetry, is accomplished,

Be welcome then, stillness of the shadow's world!
I shall be satisfied though my lyre will not
Accompany me down there. Once I
Lived like the gods, and more is not needed.[1]

—Hölderlin

Nathan Milstein, Violinist

Nathan Milstein's recital yesterday afternoon at Avery Fisher Hall was a wonder. The violinist, an incredible 74 years old, appeared on Lincoln Center's Great Performers series and reminded the large audience what that title was meant to describe. Here was playing of nobility and impeccable taste and the kind of flawless musicianship that for half a century has been a Milstein hallmark.

—Donal Henahan, music critic for The New York Times

[1]Kaufmann's translation. Kaufmann's (1976) superb analysis of Hölderlin's poem concludes that the race with death can be won. It suggested the theme for this book, and in particular the interviews with living artists.

Biography

Known as one of the greatest living violinists for his technical brilliance and stylistic nuances, Milstein was born in Russia in 1904. In 1929 he made his American debut with the St. Louis Symphony Orchestra. He made America his home-base, but continued to tour the world with major orchestras as a soloist. He has toured Russia triumphantly with Vladimir Horowitz.

Milstein's repertoire concentrates largely on Romantic composers. He has also composed and arranged violin music himself.

Interview

Though one of the most interesting interviews for its spontaneity, sense of humor, and the variety of subjects discussed, lasting well over an hour, it presented difficulties in terms of adhering to the framework of the Standard Interview questions. From the very beginning, Milstein reversed roles, asking me questions on a number of topics, relating amusing anecdotes, and appraising the state of the arts.

The following are excerpts from the "conversation stage." Blaming the relatively low level of art today on the absence of a musically educated elite who, competing with each other stimulate the arts, Milstein remarked: "Today everything is commercial. And people think that what they don't understand must be good; that goes for music as well as paintings. Most of the modern music is not *art* at all, and will not endure very long. Even Rachmaninoff will not have a longevity of more than 100 years. But 100 years is pretty good—that's a long time."

He did not seem eager to get into the main topic of the interview, as the following remark indicates:

N.M.: What a shame to talk about death. I don't mind talking about it, but I would much rather discuss other things, such as life.

I: Do you consider yourself religious?

N.M.: "Mystical" would be a better term. I completely agree with Einstein on these questions. He was a friend of mine. I still remember the first time I met him. It was at [Artur] Schnabel's house. I was a young man and at that time much more impressed at being invited to the Schnabels, such an illustrious music family, than by Einstein, who was then a relatively unknown young scientist. But to come back to religiousness; Einstein felt very strongly that there was an order or a power underlying it all, over which we have no effect. That is, he felt that men cannot effect real important changes. We can hurt mankind, but we cannot destroy it, or make any fundamental changes. I share this view.

I.: Do you feel you have accomplished what you wanted to accomplish in life? Are you satisfied, fulfilled?

N.M.: Satisfied with what I have done so far, yes. But "fulfilled" is not the correct word. That implies that I have achieved all I want to or am able to. I don't feel that I have.

I.: You mean, you feel that you are still growing or changing?

N.M.: Yes. I don't feel I have reached the peak. My satisfaction is more like "inner harmony."

I.: With respect to your artistic accomplishments?

N.M.: Of course. The important thing is that I am still changing.

I.: In the way you experience time, which time perspective is the most important one: past, present, or future?

N.M.: Certainly not the past! The past is so unimportant to me, I am not even interested in history. Present and future [are important]. Living is important.

I.: Do you mean, living every moment, being aware of time passing, of the limits of available time?

N.M.: No. That's neurotic—I am not neurotic.

I.: How long do you *expect* to live?

N.M.: I have no intuition and I am glad I don't know when I am going to die. If I knew I could no longer enjoy myself.

I.: What is your *preference*, regarding longevity? How long would you like to live?

N.M.: As long as possible, and that goes for whatever condition I am in. I would choose to survive under all circumstances.

I.: Even if you had an accident? Even if you were disabled?

N.M.: Yes, I love life, even if it means just being here.

I.: If, after you died, you could come back once, for a short period of time, when would you choose to come back: 2, 10, 100, or 1,000 years after your death?

N.M.: Not at all!

I.: Why not?

N.M.: I am not interested—no curiosity at all. In this life, yes. But it's all I want. It fulfills my needs. Does anyone say that he wants to come back?

I.: Yes. Most people say they are curious. One artist said he would be interested to find out how a young protégé of his is going to make out in the future.

N.M.: What nonsense! It's all so unimportant! They answer without really thinking it through.

I.: How about visiting a period in the past, before you were born?

N.M.: No, I would not. It must have been awful. I like today's comforts. They must have smelled badly—didn't take baths—I would have had to play with dirty hands. Imagine, even if I could meet Beethoven—it's not interesting. His music is, and we have that. But being with him—he was a cranky, disagreeable old man. There are also some *great* men alive now, but if they are disagreeable I would not be interested to be with them.

I.: Are you afraid of death?

N.M.: No. It's natural. I am not afraid of natural things. But I will tell you something: I do not fly. I feel anxious about it. But it is not fear of death. As I said, death is natural: flying is unnatural. You see, the takeoff and landing don't bother me, though I know they are the most dangerous moments of a flight. I am not afraid of a crash. It has to do with natural and unnatural motions. Up and down (takeoff and landing) are natural motions; but steady, horizontal flight is unnatural, even if one understands the physical laws involved. There is also an additional benefit in my refusal to fly: I like boats and trains, and I like the pacing that results from it.

I.: Did you ever fly?

N.M.: Yes, of course. But I won't again, if I can help it. As a matter of fact, twice I cancelled a concert tour in Japan. I just couldn't go through with it.

I.: How often do you think about your own death?

N.M.: I do not think about it. And believe me, you should do the same. Think about life, that is much more satisfying. I am not afraid of death, but there is just no need to think about it. I am never anxious, because I don't think about it.

When asked to rate the concept "death" on the semantic differential rating scale, he only glanced at the oppositional adjectives and said that the concept could not be evaluated, adding, "It is meaningless. Death is 'nothing.' I have no feelings about it." He had no difficulty rating "life," choosing exclusively positive attributes.

Alexander Schneider, Conductor, Violinist

Biography

Alexander Schneider was born in Russia in 1908. He studied with such luminaries as Pablo Casals. He traveled extensively with his own string quartet before joining the Budapest String Quartet.

In 1944 Schneider founded the Albeneri Trio chamber music concerts and organized other musical associations such as the Sonata Ensemble, the Schneider Quartet, the New School Concerts, the Israel Music Festival. He was also a guest conductor of the Boston Philharmonic, the St. Louis Symphony, the Israel Philharmonic, the Los Angeles Philharmonic, the Orchestra of the French National Radio and TV, and the Lincoln Center Mozart Festival. He participates in France's Casals Festival and in the Marlboro Music festival in Vermont. He is the first violinist to present all of Bach's unaccompanied violin pieces in a concert series.

Schneider established the Prades Festivals with Pablo Casals and the Casals Festivals in Puerto Rico. Among the many honors he received are the Elizabeth Sprague Coolidge medal for eminent services to chamber music, 1945; and the Mayor's Scroll of Appreciation, New York City, 1959.

Interview

True to his usual part as a conductor, Alexander Schneider reversed roles immediately, and very much like Nathan Milstein, started to "conduct" the interview by asking me questions. However, this was not done to avoid any topic. On the contrary, he used almost every question as a springboard for elaborating his thoughts and feelings in the broadest possible context.

Asked about his ultimate goal, he seemed, at first, to sidestep the question:

A.S.: I cannot remember life without a goal. Long before I had set any of my own, when I was a small child, my father had already definite goals for me: to become a musician. It takes an enormous amount of work and discipline— one has to give up everything else for it. I never had a real childhood. No school with schoolmates, only very little private tutoring. No ball playing. All was music. One does not see that kind of discipline today any more. It's this lack of discipline, which is at the basis of a lot of our problems today. There are a few exceptions: Young violinists and dancers. Both require an enormous amount of discipline.

I.: What is your ultimate goal now? What would you conceive as the height of fulfillment?

A.S.: I have done all I wanted to do. I am greatly concerned with the young people today. But there is not anything in terms of goals that I want to achieve.

I.: You mean, you are not trying to surpass yourself, to reach greater heights.

A.S.: Not at all! And that's not what I am concerned with. Did you read the newspaper this morning? [Referring to an item in the paper about the Middle East.] That's what I am concerned with right now. I see us headed toward another war. It must come eventually and probably should have happened already. I do not see any solution for the future. (Now! Thanks to Sadat and Begin—perhaps no more wars.)[2]

I.: How much do you think about the future? Or rather, what is the most important time dimension to you: do you live mostly in the past, the present, or the future?

A.S.: I live fully in the present. I don't think much about the future, perhaps because I don't look forward to a future. I am very pessimistic about it. I mean, not for me, but for mankind. I am happy, I had a good life. But I feel sorry for the youth. That's how I devote most of my time now—to help the young people. Now, the past, that's extremely important, because that is what made me what I am now: my present. I do think a great deal about the past. I don't live in the past, I don't want to bring it back—just for the important part it played for my life, as a whole.

I.: How long do you *expect* to live?

---

[2]Added at the time of reviewing interview for approval.

A.S.: Not very long.

I.: What is your *preference*, regarding time of death?

A.S.: I do not want to get very old. I was with Casals when he was in his nineties, and though he was lucid and functioned well, I even thought then that I do not want to become very old.

I.: Would you say that you are ready or willing to die anytime?

A.S.: Yes. I love life—I enjoy life, but I am ready to die.

I.: If after you died you could come back once, when would you choose to come back: 2, 10, 100, or 1,000 years after your death?

A.S.: But that's my question![jokingly]. I have often thought about that. I always said I would like to come back every 100 years, to see what is going on. 1,000 years would be wonderful, if they give me enough time to read up on all that happened. But just now, I would also like to come back after twenty years, to see how someone I am interested in has been making out.

I.: Well, if you can choose only one of these intervals, which one would you choose?

A.S.: 1,000 years, if they give me enough time.

I.: If you could visit a past period, before your birth, which one would you choose: two to ten years before your birth, 1900, 1700 to 1900, antiquity, or any other?

A.S.: Between 1700 and 1900—they really knew how to live well!

I.: If you created a masterpiece, would you prefer 1,000 listeners or spectators now or in 100 years?

A.S.: Now. I am not interested in fame after my death.

I.: Are you afraid of death?

A.S.: No. Not at all! That makes me think of a period in my life, a long time ago. Three of my friends and I, we each had a lethal drug, which we intended to take in case anything terrible happened to us. What I can't understand is that they didn't take it. That is, two of them had things really go wrong. One died of cancer. And none of them took the drug. I am sure I would in such a case. I hope I would. That doesn't mean that I don't like to live. I do love life. But I also feel that death holds no fear for me. I have accepted it entirely.

I.: How often do you think about your own death?

A.S.: I don't think about it. Very rarely. I know that I have to die and whenever it happens, I welcome it. But I don't think about it.

I.: What preoccupies you most on a daily basis?

A.S.: My work. That's my life.

On the semantic differential rating scale, Schneider rated the meaning of life and of death as highly positive. The only two negative adjectives he used for death were solitary and dull.

It is interesting to compare his responses to the longevity questions with Milstein's. In Schneider's case there is complete harmony between expectation and preference: he does not expect, nor does he want to get old. He even favors suicide, if the quality of life deteriorates. This is in sharp contrast to Milstein, who would choose to survive under all conditions.

Isaac Stern, Violinist

Biography

Isaac Stern was born in Russia in 1920 and brought to America as an infant. He began pianoforte lessons at the age of six, violin at eight. He made his debut with the San Francisco Symphony Orchestra when he was eleven, and by the time he was eighteen he had appeared with the Los Angeles Philharmonic as well as giving concerts in Pacific Coast cities. After his recital in New York City, Stern was regarded as a young artist of exceptional ability.

Isaac Stern has had a continual concert career as recitalist and as a soloist with major American and European orchestras. From 1950 to 1952 he participated in the Prades Festival with Pablo Casals. He has toured South America, Israel, and Australia; and in the United States, besides recording for Columbia Records, he has performed Beethoven's chamber works for the piano with Eugene Istomin and Leonard Rose.

On a less esoteric level, Isaac Stern's soundtrack-recordings for motion pictures include playing *Humoresque* (Warner Bros.), and *Fiddler on the Roof* (United Artists), as well as starring in *Tonight We Sing* (20th Century Fox), and *Journey to Jerusalem* with Leonard Bernstein.

He is a member of the National Arts Council, chairman of the board of the American–Israel Cultural Foundation, and president of Carnegie Hall.

Interview

I.S.: Dr. Goodman, you have told me that you are doing a series of interviews with creative people. As a performer, I feel there is a clear distinction between the work of the creative artist and the accomplishments of the interpretive artist. For me, the act of creation is the special, private world of a composer or writer or painter, sculptor, etcetera. Of course, the performer too must have an enormous discipline. Then one is free to exult in a recreative experience when performing at optimum. But always remembering that the real creator in music is the composer.

I.: What is it that makes critics rank you among the top living violinists? There are hundreds of musicians who excel in your discipline, who have superior technique, yet they are not thought of as great artists.

I.S.: Possibly because of a clearer perception of what someone else has created. If a performing artist is supremely sensitive to the creative spirit, he will be able to communicate. To have the skills alone is not enough. One must also have "the inner ear"—that is, a sensitive perception.

I.: I guess what you call "sensitive perception" is what gives your performance the stamp of excellence and uniqueness, which are the main qualities of a creative act.

I.S.: There is still a distinction between one who creates, the composer, and the one who interpets.

I.: Can one say that through his interpretation the performer recreates whatever the composer created, and that these recreations vary in excellence depending on the artistic abilities of the interpreter?

I.S.: Yes, one could say that.

I.: Cannot the same be said about most artists—painters, sculptors, who recreate from nature?

I.S.: To do this subject justice would take us far astray. Another discussion in itself.

I.: What do you conceive as the height of fulfillment, the ultimate goal?

I.S.: I don't know. I am still searching.

I.: Are you satisfied with your achievements?

I.S.: Well, that's comparative. There are relative degrees of achievement. There is a degree of satisfaction for past achievements. But I cannot say that I have achieved what I want. I am only too aware of what I have not yet done. Happily, in the interpretive search there is never an end.

I.: How do you experience time? I mean, do you feel most involved with the past, present, or future?

I.S.: I can't say. There is no separation in my experience between past, present, and future. Without my past I couldn't be where I am now in the present or where I hope to go in the future. And if I had known then what I know now, I would not be me.

I.: Are you keenly aware of time passing, of the limited time available?

I.S.: No, not at all. It's relative. I look at my "old" friend, X, who is in his sixties, and at my "young" friend, Arthur Rubinstein, who is more than ninety years old. Time is relative. It can't be measured by years. It depends on the person and on one's attitude. Everybody is different.

I.: If, after you died, you could come back once, for a short period of time, when would you choose to come back: 2, 10, 100, or 1,000 years after your death?

I.S.: [emphatically] Not at all!

I.: Why not?

I.S.: [jokingly] *"Après moi, le déluge."* No, seriously, I am just not interested.

I.: If you could visit a past period, which one would you choose: two to ten years before your birth, around 1900, 1700 to 1900, antiquity, or any other?

I.S.: I have never given it serious thought.

I.: Why not?

I.S.: Well, if I really had to choose, then in the 1920's.

I.: But that was not before your birth.

I.S.: For all practical purposes it was. I wasn't aware yet of what was going on in music. And it was one of the richest periods of musical creativity in this or any other century.

I.: Are you afraid of death?

I.S.: No! It's like asking if I am afraid of a performance. I am nervous every time I perform. Only a child or a fool would not be. But why worry about it before? I don't think about it until the last ten minutes. It's the same with death. I hardly ever think about it.

I.: You hardly ever think about your own death?

I.S.: That's right. I certainly don't welcome death; the later it comes, the better. But when it comes, it comes.

Beveridge Webster, Pianist

Biography

One of the outstanding pianists of the twentieth century, Beveridge Webster has enjoyed a versatile career at the piano. Besides introducing new works by Sessions, Copland, and Carter, he has recorded much of the music by the modern composers: Berg, Webern, Schoenberg, and Stravinsky. He is also regarded as a highly-gifted interpreter of French Impressionistic music.

Webster studied in France with Isidor Philipp and Nadia Boulanger, and he was the first American to win first prize at the Paris Conservatoire. He was a frequent co-recitalist with Maurice Ravel at the home of Debussy's publisher. Between 1926 and 1938, he toured Europe and studied German composers with Artur Schnabel. His American debut came in 1934 with the New York Philharmonic on an all-American program—the first of his lifelong commitment to American music. With major orchestras, Webster has played as a soloist with such conductors as Koussevitsky, Ormandy, Klemperer, and Stravinsky.

Mr. Webster was also a commentator of contemporary music on the Voice of America broadcasts. In 1962 he received an honorary degree of Doctor of Music from the University of New Hampshire. He has served on the piano faculty of the Julliard School of Music. Webster has also recorded on major record labels.

Harold Schonberg of *The New York Times* wrote:

> An experienced, imaginative artist. He played with tremendous authority, always the complete master. The logic, the sensitivity, the power when necessary, the absolute control—all marked a pianist at the height of his powers.

Interview

This was one of the longest interviews, lasting for almost two hours, not because Webster was eager to talk about death, but because of his attempts to avoid the topic altogether. Sidetracking questions, very much like Milstein and Doktor did, he gave fascinating accounts of his own and his family's musical accomplishments.

I.: What do you consider the height of fulfillment, the ultimate goal?

B.W.: In terms of . . .?

I.: Your professional or your personal life: such as achieving higher levels in performance, recognition, fame, wealth, a good family life. What's the most important?

B.W.: I cannot choose one. They are all interrelated. Being *appreciated*, gaining *recognition*, is very important and is of course related to professional achievements. But I can't conceive of any of these without a happy family life. Or the extraordinary stimulating contact I have daily with so many brilliantly gifted young people—probably the most important feature of my present professional and personal life.

I.: Would you be willing to make great sacrifices for the sake of success, recognition—to attain whatever is important to you?

B.W. I always liked what I was doing be it teaching, practicing, performing. It never felt like making sacrifices.

I.: In your experience of time, which seems to be your most important time dimension: past, present, or future?

B.W.: In my experience, time is not divided in terms of past, present, and future. It is much more unified. Of course, technically, there is no present. I am also aware of the greatly reduced future, as compared to my past.

I.: Do you wish you could bring back the past—do you live mostly in the past?

B.W.: Not at all.

I.: How long do you *expect* to live?

B.W.: I have no intuition whatsoever. I just know that at sixty-five it is limited. I don't have another sixty-five years left.

I.: What is your *preference* regarding time of death?

B.W.: None really. I appreciate every daily postponement.

I.: The later the better?

B.W.: Yes, as long as I function well.

I.: If after you died you could come back once for a short period, when would you choose to come back: 2, 10, 100, or 1,000 years after your death?

B.W.: Never! I am not interested at all in coming back. Perhaps remaining alive (immortality) could be a choice, but that too would be a catastrophe.

I.: If you could visit a period in the past which would you choose: two to ten years before your birth, 1900, 1700 to 1900, antiquity, or any other?

B.W.: None. I have no desire to visit a past period. History is already too complicated as it is.

I.: If you could create a masterpiece, perhaps in terms of recording, would you prefer 1,000 listeners now or in 100 years?

B.W.: I would prefer to know that people in 100 years will listen to my records. Perhaps that's easy for me to say, since I have the audience now.

I.: Are you afraid of death?

B.W.: Yes, of dying painfully. I am not afraid of being dead. Death itself could be welcome. What I am afraid of is the process of dying. I deeply pity and care for those subjected to a slow painful death, particularly the death of a loved one, or a once-loved one.

I.: How often do you think of your own death: daily, once a week, hardly ever?

B.W.: I think of my impending death, but I can't say how often. Probably once a week would come close to it. (jokingly) Never on Sundays.

Paul Doktor, Violist

Biography

Born in 1919, he studied the violin with his father Karl, who was co-founder of and a violist with the Busch Quartet. Paul Doktor graduated from the State Academy of Music in Vienna in 1938 and played the viola with the Busch Quartet and the Adolph Busch Chamber Orchestra. From 1940 until 1947 he was first violist with the Lucerne Symphony and with the Collegium Musicum. In 1948 he made his American debut in Washington, D.C., at the Library of Congress.

From 1948 until 1951 he was a violist and guest lecturer of the faculty string quartet at the University of Michigan in Ann Arbor.

Since 1952 he has served on the faculty of Mannes College of Music in New York. He has toured throughout the United States, Canada, and Europe in recital and with orchestras. Doktor founded the Rococo Ensemble and the New York String Sextet.

In 1942 he won first prize at the International Music Competition in Geneva, Switzerland.

Interview

Paul Doktor was very gracious about granting me an interview, but he
made it immediately clear that he would very much prefer not to talk
about death. He is an excellent conversationalist, and his accounts of
his musical career, his travels, his early association with the Busch
Quartet and with many other illustrious musicians made the task of
asking specific interview questions somewhat difficult. I did, however,
manage eventually to ask about his ultimate goal.

P.D.: That has always remained the same, from my early childhood
on—to be a musician *of reputation.*

I.: How important is that now? I mean, would you be willing to make
great sacrifices for the sake of your work?

P.D.: I have never made any sacrifices—I never had to give up anything.
I always did what I wanted to do, and had a very good time doing it.

I.: I mean very hard work, abstain from anything that may interfere with
it.

P.D.: Well, it just doesn't work like this. I don't feel I have ever had to
sacrifice anything, or had to abstain from having a good time. But I have also
worked hard. If I study a new piece, I may stay up all night, if necessary. That
has happened. But I don't consider that a sacrifice, or giving up anything. I
want to do that—it's part of my life.

I.: Which time dimension is most important to you, the past, present, or
future?

P.D.: I am mostly present-oriented. But I am also looking toward the
future.

I.: How long do you expect to live?

P.D.: Very long—into old age.

I.: What is your preference regarding time of death?

P.D.: Reach old age—the later the better.

I.: If after you died you could come back once for a short period, when
would you choose to come back: 2, 10, 100, or 1,000 years after your death?

P.D.: Ten is too soon, but 100 is too far off. I would be interested to see a
period which is still in touch with our own time. More like twenty-five to fifty
years after.

I.: Well, if you don't have that choice, which do you prefer?

P.D.: I guess 100 years is more interesting.

I.: If you created a masterpiece, would you prefer a 1,000 spectators or listeners now or in 100 years?

P.D.: Now.

I.: Are you afraid of death?

P.D.: No. I don't think so. But I don't want it to catch me unaware. I have too many loose ends. That's why I don't even want to think about it. There is so much unfinished business—so much in disorder. I don't want to leave that mess behind. I am just not ready for it. I haven't accomplished all that I could accomplish. When I said that I am not afraid of death, I mean I am not preoccupied with it. For instance, I don't hesitate to fly. I fly all the time. If I were afraid of death, I wouldn't fly. But if I were told that I will die tomorrow, that may be another thing—perhaps I would be afraid.

I.: How often do you think of your own death?

P.D.: I don't think about it. Very rarely.

On the semantic differential rating scale, Paul Doktor rated the meaning of death as slightly negative and the meaning of life as highly positive. The negative characteristics he attributed to death were solitary, violent, chaotic, and worthless.

Vladimir Ashkenazy, Pianist

Biography

Born in Russia in 1937, Ashkenazy is known as one of the finest pianists of his generation with his gift of an imaginative and lyrical style. He made his debut at the age of seven, playing a Haydn concerto. In 1955 he won second prize at the International Chopin Competition in Warsaw. After studying for ten years at the Central Music School in Moscow, he entered the Moscow State Conservatory.

In Brussels, Ashkenazy took first prize at the Queen Elizabeth Competition in 1956. And it was in 1958 that he made his American debut. Ashkenazy continued to amass honors and acclaim. In 1962 he was the joint winner with John Ogdon at the Tchaikovsky Piano Competition in Moscow. In 1971 he was awarded the Icelandic Order of the Falcon.

Interview

I.: Do you feel you have achieved or are achieving what you really wanted in life?

V.A.: No. Does anyone?

I.: What do you mean?

V.A.: Well, the moment I have achieved what I wanted, there is something else, a new goal. For instance, when I was a teenager, I wanted to be famous—which is rather commonplace at that age. That's unimportant now.

I.: Do you experience satisfaction, fulfillment, now?

V.A.: I am satisfied with the kind of life I am leading; that is, with my whole life-style—I am doing what I want to do professionally—and with my personal life, my children, my wife. But feeling fulfilled? No—that would be the end; I would be finished.

I.: Do you mean you are still changing—searching?

V.A.: Yes, of course.

I.: What is your ultimate goal?

V.A.: I don't know—what do you mean?

I.: Well, you said that once it was fame, recognition. What about wealth? Material things?

V.A.: No, not at all. None of these things.

I.: Achieving higher levels of functioning? Creating?

V.A.: Yes, of course.

I.: How do you experience time? I mean which time dimension is the most important one to you: past, present, or future?

V.A.: Well, you know there is really no present, it's always past or future. But I don't dwell on the past. I must look ahead to the future—even concerts are planned for at least two years ahead, if we speak in practical terms. But in my performances it is the present that is of the utmost importance. I know that there are some people for whom it is all ONE—they are very sensitive—like almost experiencing their future in the present. I am not that sensitive. I am really very ordinary.

I.: Do you have any preference as to the time of your death—

V.A.: [interrupting] "I am ready any time. I love life, but I think I am ready to die, whenever. One must be.

I.: Imagine that after you have died you could come back once, for a short period of time. When would you choose to come back: 2, 10, 100, or 1,000 years after your death?

V.A.: [Is amused, laughs, but doesn't answer.]

I.: Well, do you want to come back?

V.A.: [jokingly] If it's offered, why not? After 100 years. Two and ten is much too short—not enough changes. 1,000 years is to late—we can't relate to it anymore. But 100 is interesting.

I.: Why would you want to come back then?

V.A.: Out of curiosity. Just see what's going on.

I.: If you could visit a period in the past, which one would you choose: two to ten years before your birth, 1900, 1700 to 1900, antiquity, or any other?

V.A.: If it is also just for a short period, if I don't have to live in it, ancient Greece. I am interested in ancient Greece, and I would like to see if the Greeks were any different from us or similar to us. I kind of think they were really very much like us. It would be interesting to confirm. Human nature is probably the same over any period of time. What do you think?

I.: I agree. Now imagine that you are not famous and you had a choice: either 1,000 listeners now, *or* in 100 years. Which would you choose?

V.A.: It makes no difference.

I.: You mean it's equally important to you?

V.A.: No. It's not important; it's the same. If you know that what you are doing is right, it doesn't matter when others recognize it; even if they never do. Fame doesn't matter at all in this particular respect—just to know that what I am doing is good. It is an inner feeling and what I consider truth in art is almost impossible to explain in words.

I.: I would like you to complete the story: "Joe has a cup of coffee in a restaurant. He is thinking of the time to come when . . . " [M. Wallace, 1956].

V.A.: [amused] That's just like things you hear on T.V. What do you want me to say? The first thing that comes to mind? I could answer it as a joke; or do you want me to take it seriously?

I.: Yes, take it seriously, but answer whatever you want; whatever comes to your mind.

V.A.: Well, you see, if I am Joe, I don't think seriously in a restaurant, having a cup of coffee. I think seriously when I am alone, just sitting, thinking, or alone with my wife. But I would say that he is thinking of the time to come when he will have inner peace.

I.: Are you afraid of death?

V.A.: No!

I.: Why not?

V.A.: [laughing] *Why not*?! Because it's natural. I guess no one has complete equanimity about death, but I don't fear it. It's a natural thing.

I.: Are you preoccupied with it? I mean do you think often about your own death?

V.A.: Yes, very frequently.

On the semantic differential rating scale, Ashkenazy rated the meaning of both "death" and "life" as slightly negative.

Alan Arkin, Actor, Director, Writer, Composer

> . . . the extraordinarily fine and winning performance of Alan Arkin, as a New York Puerto Rican determined to wrest his two young sons from a slum ghetto, moves this brilliantly versatile actor forward in the tradition of the great movie comedians. Yes, such as Chaplin.

—*Howard Thompson*, The New York Times, *on Arkins' role as Popi in the movie of the same name.*

Biography

Actor, director, writer, and composer, Alan Arkin was born in New York City in 1934. He studied at Los Angeles City College, 1951–53, and Bennington College, 1953–55.

Mr. Arkin made his New York City theater debut in *From the Second City* and subsequently appeared in *Man Out Loud, Girl Quiet* for which he also composed the music. In 1963 he received the Antoinette Perry (Tony) Award and won the New York Drama Critics Poll for his portrayal of David Kolovitz in *Enter Laughing*.

His motion picture credits include *Wait Until Dark, The Heart Is a Lonely Hunter, Little Murders, The Russians Are Coming, The Russians are Coming, Catch-22, Last of the Red Hot Lovers, The Seven Percent Solution,* and *The In-Laws*, in which he co-stars with Peter Falk.

Interview

Talking about his accomplishments in a very unassuming manner, Alan Arkin feels that his successes have gone far beyond his aspirations. He is not hoping or striving for higher levels of achievement, feeling that he can never surpass Renoir's directing nor his own present performance as an actor.

A.A.: I am happy with my life as it is. I like what I am doing—I like my family life—I will never live in a more beautiful house—there isn't anything I would want to change. I am not running after things, I just let them happen.

I.: What do you conceive as the ultimate goal, the height of fulfillment?

A.A.: To forget about myself completely. It's difficult to put into words. Not to be self-conscious—to be free of self-involvement.

I.: Does that happen when one is so involved in one's work that one loses oneself?

A.A.: It can happen anywhere. On the stage, playing tennis—it doesn't matter. It is a peak experience. It does happen more and more often to me.

I.: How do you experience time? I mean, which time dimension is the most important to you: past, present, or future?

A.A.: At one time I was all future-directed; now much more present. The past, not at all [important].

I.: Are you overwhelmingly aware of time passing, of the limits of available time?

A.A.: No.

I.: How long do you expect to live?

A.A.: Oh, well into the seventies.

I.: What is your preference regarding longevity?

A.A.: Around 105 years.

I.: The later, the better?

A.A.: Yes! I like to be around.

I.: If after you died you could come back once for a short period, when would you choose to come back: 2, 10, 100, or 1,000 years after your death?

A.A.: That would depend on when I die. If I died right now, I would want to see what happened to my children. I would say in ten years. If I died in old age, I would say 100 years, or perhaps not at all.

I.: How about choosing one of these intervals.

A.A.: I really can't say.

I.: If you could visit a past period, before you were born, which would you choose: two to ten years before your birth, around 1900, 1700 to 1900, antiquity, or any other?

A.A.: Antiquity.

I.: Why?

A.A.: Because of my interest in Egyptian civilization.

I.: Are you afraid of death?

A.A.: No. I am not hanging on to my life. I love life, and once I was afraid of death, but now I can let go. Since I have done "my thing" I am no longer afraid of death. I have also studied yoga for five years, which is, in a sense the study of dying. I rarely think about my own death now.

I.: What does "rarely" mean? Once a week, once a month, hardly ever?

A.A.: Hardly ever.

I.: If you create a masterpiece, what would you prefer: 1,000 readers or spectators now, or in 100 years?

A.A.: It doesn't make any difference. I am only concerned with being good. A few people are important to me now, but I do not have the need to be appreciated by thousands, now or later.

On the semantic differential rating scale, Alan Arkin rated the meaning of death and the meaning of life positively. The only negative characteristic he attributed to death was "solitary."

Eva Le Gallienne, Actress, Writer

Biography

One of the truly great ladies of the American theater, Eva Le Gallienne came to this country at age sixteen, having made her professional debut in London the year before. She played her first starring role in

Liliom in 1921, followed by another triumph in Molnar's *The Swan*. In 1926 she founded the Civic Repertory Theatre, which became the most successful repertory company this country has seen to this day. Miss LeGallienne acted, directed, produced, and managed it for eight years, presenting over forty of the world's classics. In 1947 she co-founded the American Repertory Theatre, with which she starred and directed. After touring the United States and Canada as Queen Elisabeth in Schiller's *Mary Stuart*, she spent several years touring with the National Repertory Theatre. She has also been associated with the American Shakespeare Festival at Stratford in her dual capacity of actress/director. In 1975 Miss Le Gallienne again won rave reviews and awards for her portrayal of Fanny Cavendish in the Broadway revival of *The Royal Family*. After a season on Broadway she played the role on a national tour and filmed the performance for Public Television. Le Gallienne recently completed *Resurrection*, a new Universal film with Ellen Burstyn.

Eva Le Gallienne is also an author. Her publications include two personal memoirs: *At 33* and *With A Quiet Heart*; a children's book, *Flossie and Bossie*; and *The Mystic in the Theatre*, a study of Eleonora Duse. She has translated Ibsen's plays and the tales of Hans Christian Andersen. At present Crowell, Harper and Row, is publishing her translation of Carl Evald's nature tales, *The Spider and Other Stories*.

Miss Le Gallienne has been the recipient of literally dozens of honorary degrees and awards, and she especially appreciates the Norwegian Grand Cross of the Royal Order of St. Olaf.

Interview

It was on a clear cold winter day that I drove to Le Gallienne's country home in New England. A very agile, "young" woman came to meet me outside to lead me to the main house. She looked just as I remembered her, from many, many years ago; but not just beautiful or graceful— she is most strikingly in tune with her surroundings, in perfect harmony with them. As we passed an old barn and a gazebo, she remarked that this place, looking and smelling like the English countryside, has been her home for over fifty years. Inside the house a woodfire was burning in the fireplace. A huge snow-white cat was sleeping on the windowsill. The walls were lined with books—beautiful leather-bound books from floor to ceiling.

Le Gallienne knew that she was the first of all the famous women I had contacted to agree to be interviewed and she was wondering why so many others had declined. I suggested that perhaps superstition, so prevalent in performers, may even be stronger in women than in men and account for their greater reluctance to talk about death. She remarked that, indeed, when she had told a friend about our impending interview, the friend did not like the idea at all and had tried to persuade her not to go ahead with it.

Of all the interviews I had conducted with celebrities and with noncelebrities, this was the first time that I found myself hesitant to get into the interview proper. Not because of the subject matter, not because there was any reluctance in my interviewee (which I had so frequently observed in others). It was I who wanted to learn and to linger on other aspects of life. We did speak about the theater and about great artists, with Le Gallienne's views backed up in a delightful way by the most fitting quotes of the great poets. Somehow, Eleonora Duse kept coming to my mind. I asked Le Gallienne if she had ever seen her. Yes, she had seen Duse in a number of plays. And yes, she was the greatest! But not a word about their relationship. Only when I was leaving Le Gallienne presented me with a little book: *The Mystic in the Theatre: Eleanora Duse* by Eva Le Gallienne.

I was startled to discover that the two great artists, Le Gallienne, then a young new star at the beginning of a long career, and the aging, ailing Duse, yet undisputably at the peak of her stardom to the very end, shared a deep personal relationship. The very last message Duse had sent before her death was a telegram to Le Gallienne.

I.: Do you have an *ultimate* goal in life?

Le G.: Yes. Every artist does. Not that I have achieved it! It really can't be reached. Leonardo had already observed man's greatest tragedy: "Theory outstrips performance."

I.: Does that mean that the goal is "perfection"?

Le G.: Perfection in terms of performance—in terms of art.

I.: What would you do for its sake, for the sake of reaching it?

Le G.: Anything! My profession has been the passion of my life. I would sacrifice everything for it. As a matter of fact, I *have* [done so].

I.: What is your most important time orientation. I mean, do you stress most the past, the present, or the future?

Le G.: I cannot say. They are all one. I can't divide the part that is past from the present or future. As you get older time ceases to exist in this way. Six years ago is like the day before yesterday. There is no measurement. It's just there. It's all there.

I.: Are you nostalgic about the past?

Le G.: No!

I.: Do you live a great deal in the past—do you wish you could bring it back?

Le G.: Not at all! I am much more forward looking.

I.: How long do you expect to live?

Le G.: I have no idea.

I.: What is your preference in terms of the time of your death?

Le G.: It doesn't matter. Whenever it happens.

I.: If after you died you could come back once for a short period, when would you choose to come back: 2, 10, 100, or 1,000 years after your death?

Le G.: A hundred.

I.: Why?

Le G.: The most extraordinary things have happened in my lifetime, in the last eighty years. I remember the day when mother took us to Orly, to see the "machine" land—that was the beginning of air travel. And I can still see, in front of my eyes, one of the first automobiles [described its appearance to the most minute details]; it belonged to Arnold Bennett, who was a friend of my mother. It could go fifteen miles an hour, and nanny would simply not believe that such speed was humanly possible. And then there was the radio, and television—so many incredible changes crammed into 80 years. It would be interesting to see if so many new things can happen again within the next 100 years.

I.: If you could visit a past period, which one would you choose: two to ten years before your birth, 1700 to 1900, antiquity, or any other?

Le G.: The Elizabethan Period.

I.: I guess for obvious reasons: literature, theater . . .

Le G.: No. Simply because I love her [Elizabeth I].

I.: I don't think Schiller liked her very much. Do you know his *Maria Stuart*?

Le G.: Yes, of course. I played Elisabeth in it, many times.

I.: Schiller's heroine is really Maria Stuart. He loves her.

Le G.: Yes, I know. But she was really foolish. By the way, you know that Elisabeth and Maria Stuart never met face to face. Schiller's isn't real historical.

I.: Are you afraid of death?

Le G.: I don't think so. Of course this is something one cannot know for sure, but I don't feel any fear. It's part of life, part of the rhythm of the universe. And I am not a believer, so I don't fear anything that may come afterwards. I don't think that there is anything. Going to sleep is certainly not frightening. The very best thing is just going to sleep—eternal sleep. Remember, " . . . 'tis a consummation/Devoutly to be wish'd."

I.: How often do you think about your own death?

Le G.: Very seldom. Every now and then. For instance, when someone says something like, "In five years you should . . . " I think, "who knows where I am going to be in five years."

If given the choice of living her life in her own period or in a past or future one, Le Gallienne would choose her own period.

The idea of science banishing death entirely holds no appeal to her. Interestingly, her misgivings at mankind dabbling with the existing order, rhythm, renewal of life as we know it, are not simply born out of a distrust in our capabilities; almost to the contrary: she is fully aware of our extraordinary resourcefulness and our ability to effect changes. But these are not the human qualities Le Gallienne appreciates, stating: "It is man's wisdom I admire, not his *cleverness*. I love life, our finite life with its eternal renewal; not our skill in manipulating nature."

On the semantic differential rating scale, Le Gallienne ascribed exclusively positive terms to life and to death.

Alton Tobey, Painter, Illustrator

Biography

Born in 1914, Alton Tobey—painter and illustrator—received a BFA and MFA at the Yale University School of Fine arts. Tobey's works are represented in permanent collections in Sweden, Denmark, France,

Israel, Peru, Guatemala, and the U.S. He has executed murals for the Smithsonian Museum of Natural History and the McArthur Memorial in Norfolk, Virginia. His works have also been exhibited at the Wadsworth Athenium, the National Academy, and on ABC-TV, among others.

Tobey's portraits include those of Douglas MacArthur, Robert Frost, Golda Meir, Arturo Toscanini, Albert Einstein, and Alexander Calder. He has found time to teach—at Yale and at the City College of New York. At present, he directs the Artist's Equity of New York.

Interview

The interview took place in Tobey's home, surrounded by his works of art. He was as enthusiastic explaining his development and changing preoccupation in art as in discussing his views on death.

I.: What is your ultimate goal?

A.T.: In terms of *personal* self-fulfillment? I don't think there is *a* goal?

I.: How important is that to you? I mean how much would you be willing to sacrifice, for the sake of your work?

A.T.: I have, at times, been absorbed in my work to the point of complete self-oblivion. Once I worked for thirty-six hours without a break—to complete exhaustion; and while I was in the middle of it I didn't even notice. I simply could not stop—I had to finish it. There are times one just can't interrupt. I will take physical punishment if the work requires it. But one isn't even always aware of it. There are times one is so absorbed that one is simply oblivious to everything else. I can be so involved that I am no longer conscious of my needs or even of any pains. But there have also been times when I felt the exhaustion—when it was physically painful, but I just couldn't stop. But that is not the rule. I don't normally work like that; but it does happen.

I.: I would like you to assess the way you experience time. Which time dimension seems the most important to you: past, present, or future?

A.T.: I have a very poor sense of time past; on the other hand, I have a great sense of time passing by. I have both, great appreciation of the present and of the future.

I.: Do you mean by "great sense of time passing by" awareness of the limited time that is available?

A.T.: Exactly. I am keenly aware of it.

I.: How long do you expect to live?

A.T.: A relatively short time.

I.: What would be your preference, regarding time of your death?

A.T.: The later the better.

I.: If you could come back once after you died, when would you choose to come back: 2, 10, 100, or 1,000 years after your death?

A.T.: A thousand years, of course. I can still imagine what the world will be like in 100 years. To see it in 1,000 years would be far more interesting.

I.: If you could visit a past period, before your birth, which one would you choose: two to ten years before your birth, around 1900, 1700 to 1900, antiquity, or any other period?

A.T.: During the Renaissance. I guess the reasons are obvious, for an artist.

I.: Would you prefer 1,000 people seeing a masterpiece of yours now, or in 100 years?

A.T.: In 100 years. I like the idea of leaving something to posterity.

I.: Are you afraid of death?

A.T.: No! Not at all! Sometimes I would welcome it. I am not afraid of death, but what is frightening is to have no experience or no thoughts left, being a vegetable. But it is only frightening if one has a residual memory—that is, when one is still alive. Death itself is "nothing"; of that I have no fear.

I.: How often do you think about your death?

A.T.: Indirectly I must be greatly aware of it, since I am so aware of the limited time I have available. Directly I think of it only at times when something is physically wrong with me—like having a tooth pulled. At such moments I feel like "here goes a part of myself, that's dying."

I.: Do you think you may be avoiding thinking about death *directly*?

A.T.: I do not avoid any thought, wherever it may take me. To me, death is the great motivator in all creative achievements. I mean our knowledge of our death. I am certain that Da Vinci or Michelangelo could only have done what they did, I mean the trying, exhausting, physically painful work, because they were motivated to leave their work to posterity. But that's only one aspect of it; the other is that we know we don't have forever. We must do it now. That is really what I mean by "death as the great motivator."

On the semantic differential rating scale, Tobey evaluated both "death" and "life" slightly positively. The only negative adjective he attributed to the meaning of death was "solitary," while he attributed "violent, cruel, chaotic" to the meaning of life.

William King, Sculptor

Biography

William King, an artist and sculptor, was born in Florida in 1925. He studied at the University of Florida before attending the Cooper Union Art School from 1945 to 1948, where he won the Sculpture Prize. In 1949 he studied at the Brooklyn Museum Art School, and that year he was awarded a Fulbright Grant.

His artworks have been exhibited at places such as the Philadelphia Museum, 1949; Brandeis University Art Gallery, 1965; Los Angeles County Museum, 1966; University of California Art Gallery, 1966; and the Guggenheim, 1966.

His commissions have included murals for the S.S. *United States*; sculpture for SUNY at Fredonia, Potsdam, and New Paltz. King's works belong to the art collections of the Rockefellers, John Hay Whitney, Walter Chrysler, J. H. Hirshhorn, Mrs. A. List, Cornell University, Brandeis, University of California at Berkeley, Dartmouth, N.Y.U., among many others.

He has won the Augustus St. Gaudens Medal of Cooper Union, the Margaret Tiffany Blake Fresco Award, and the 1974 Creative Artists Public Service Award and Grant.

Interview

The interview took place in King's loft. It is the most atypical of those conducted with creative artists. There was no conversation stage at the beginning or at the end. King answered questions as monosyllabically as possible, without ever looking up from his work. For the most part his responses do not seem to reflect his own feelings but a set moral code of "shoulds." In his fatalistic, passive view of life, happenings are entirely outside his control: One does what one "should" be doing, and one dies when one "should" be dying.

I.: What do you want out of life? What do you conceive as your ultimate goal?

W.K.: To be able to do what I want to do and what I should be doing.

I.: Is there anything specific you want to do or achieve?

W.K.: No, I can't say. I just want to go on doing what I know I should do.

I.: How far would you be willing to go, or to sacrifice, to be able to go on doing your thing?

W.K.: I can't say—it's no sacrifice as long as you can do what you want to do.

I.: What is your most important time dimension? Do you live mostly in the past, the present, or the future?

W.K.: No, I don't make that distinction. I experience time more like a unity. But I am acutely aware of the limits of available time.

I.: How long do you *expect* to live?

W.K.: To old age.

I.: What is your *preference*, regarding time of death?

W.K.: I have no preference. Whenever it's going to happen is when it should happen. At the correct time.

I.: What or when is the correct time?

W.K.: Whenever it happens.

I.: If after you died you could come back once for a short period of time, when would you choose to come back: 2, 10, 100, or 1,000 years after your death?

W.K.: I am not sure I would like to come back at all.

I.: Why not?

W.K.: Well, I believe that one returns anyway—or rather, one goes to another place that can only be better than this life on earth. My mother already taught me that the worst hell is the one here, on earth. No, I have no desire to come back at all.

I.: If you could visit a period in the past, a period before your birth, which one would you choose: two to ten years before your birth, 1900, 1700 to 1900, antiquity, or any other?

W.K.: None! I am not interested in visiting the past.

I.: What is more important to you: 1,000 people admiring your work now or in 100 years from now?

W.K.: Now.

I.: Are you afraid of death?

W.K.: Yes.

I.: What about death do you fear?

W.K.: The unknown.

I.: How often do you think about your own death?

W.K.: Oh, not too often. Once in a while.

I.: Like once a week?

W.K.: More like once a month.

On the semantic differential rating scale, King rated "death" as highly positive, ascribing not a single negative quality to that concept. His overall rating of "life" was slightly positive.

At the conclusion I asked whether the interview had affected him in any way.

W.K.: Yes, it makes me feel uncomfortable.

I.: Can you say what about it makes you feel uncomfortable?

W.K.: Yes—it's like realizing that it is going to happen. It may not even be so far off. The most uncomfortable, the worst is to waste one's life.

Lawrence Beall Smith, Painter, Sculptor

Biography

Lawrence Beall Smith, painter and sculptor, was born in Washington, D.C., in 1909. He graduated Phi Beta Kappa from the University of Chicago and subsequently studied with Ernest Thurn, Charles Hopkinson, and Harold Zimmerman.

His work has taken him to Brandeis, Harvard, the University of Chicago, the Library of Congress, the Metropolitan Museum of Art, the Fogg Museum in Cambridge, and the Whitney Museum in New

York, where he has had an exhibit. In addition, he has illustrated works by Ogden Nash, Henry Fielding, Henry James, and Edith Wharton, among others.

Interview

The interview was conducted in the artist's studio. Lawrence Beall Smith seemed to enjoy talking about his work, showing and explaining the sculptures and paintings he was working on.

Talking about his life's goal, he said:

L.B.S.: I am very tied up with family life, that's very important, but I can't imagine being anything else but an artist. My whole life-style has to conform to my work. I am totally committed to it. My goal is to continue doing what I am doing.

I.: Which time dimension is the most important to you: past, present, or future?

L.B.S.: I don't think much about the past. The present is the most important. I also feel some pressure about the present. Things that have to be done, *now*.

I.: How long do you expect to live?

L.B.S. Into old age.

I.: What is your preference, regarding time of death?

L.B.S.: The same. To die in old age.

I.: If after you died you could come back once for a short period, when would you choose to come back: 2, 10, 100, or 1,000 years after your death?

L.B.S.: Ten years. To see the continuation of my family.

I.: If you could visit a past period, which one would you choose: two to ten years before your birth, 1900, 1700 to 1900, antiquity, or any other?

L.B.S.: Antiquity. That is the most interesting for any artist.

I.: If you created a masterpiece, what would you prefer: 1,000 spectators now or in 100 years?

L.B.S.: Now.

I.: Are you afraid of death?

L.B.S.: No. As a matter of fact, death fascinates me. I like thinking and talking about it. I do not fear it.

I.: How often do you think about your own death?

L.B.S.: Very frequently. At my age one is very aware of it.

I.: Do you think you would sacrifice your life for a great cause, for a person, or for anything?

L.B.S.: Yes, for a person.

I.: If you knew you had only one year to live, would you make any changes in your life-style?

L.B.S.: No, I am sure I would not make any changes.

On the semantic differential rating scale, Lawrence Beall Smith rated the meaning of death and of life as highly positive. He did, however, evaluate death as slightly solitary and desperate in addition to fair, kind, gentle, stimulating, harmonious, and valuable.

5

Analysis of Artists' Responses

Performing Artist Versus the Visual Artist

Some interesting field-related differences between the performing and nonperforming artists do emerge. In contrast to the performing artists, the painters or sculptors interviewed did not seem to be striving for ever higher levels of accomplishment or for an ultimate goal. Rather, they expressed the desire to continue to do just what they had been doing. Instead of vertical movement toward a peak, one gets the impression of an even, horizontal expansion.

These differences might be related to the relative permanency of various artistic works. Performing artists, even if they "sing like the gods," to paraphrase Hölderlin, leave no concrete, visual mark. No trace of their genius remains other than in the memory of listeners or on recordings, both rather ephemeral instruments. And since performers gain little satisfaction by contemplating their completed works, the height of fulfillment may lie in constant attempts to surpass themselves.

This is where the real difference between the performer and all other artists lies. Performing artists are not less "creative," as Isaac Stern seemed to imply. It is just that their artistic accomplishment is restricted to that very moment in which they are artistically engaged. Creativity for a performing artist is an *act* rather than an object and requires constant renewal. Thus, while a feeling of completion can be achieved in the *present moment,* it remains ephemeral, and the performer reorients her/himself toward the future, continuing to strive for another goal . . . and another beyond that. . . . This passionate striving which pulls the artist forward, combined with moments of extraordinary gratification, may be factors in a phenomenon that has recently come to the attention of gerontologists and psychologists: the remarkable professional longevity of so many great performing musicians, such as Casals, Heifetz, Horowitz, Milstein, Rubinstein, Stokowski.

The Artist's Syndrome

One way of assessing whether our highly self-actualized group of artists has come to terms with finiteness any better than less self-actualized individuals is, of course, by comparing critical responses of the respective groups. But to do that we first need to consider some of the unexpected reactions shown in response style as well as in content, which reveal a remarkable homogeneity *within* the artist group. Since they recur repeatedly and almost exclusively in these interviews, they are referred to as the "artist's syndrome."

Response Style: Resistance to Conformity

It has been pointed out that both Milstein and Schneider by-passed the usual interviewer–respondent relationship and, reversing roles, "conducted" their interviews. Still more common was the artists' refusal to respond to specific questions or to pick any of the multiple choices that were suggested. The artists ignored imposed categories and instead created their own alternatives. Stern's interview is a prototype of the artist's resistance to conformity. He reacts to any kind of restraint inherent in specific questions by first negating the question and by challenging the underlying concepts. Only after he has thus removed the limits imposed by the question does he express his thoughts and feelings. Thus, he immediately objects to being labeled a creative artist; he *cannot* say what his ultimate goal is; he *cannot* choose his most dominant time orientation; he is *not* interested in the past, *nor* in the future. He is *not* afraid of death, *nor* does he think about it.

But this apparent negativism is not simply a question of response style. There is also an astonishing agreement in the artists' chosen alternatives, lending further support to the notion of an artist's syndrome.

Time as "Unity"

The artists' personal time orientation is largely multidimensional, with the present embracing both past and future. A number of artists claim outright that they experience no separation between past, present, and future.[1] Others are less aware of this "unified" experience of time, but they too reject the idea of a single, most dominant time perspective. Interestingly, Schneider denies any preoccupation with the future when directly confronted with the question, but despite his negations, involvement with the future manifests itself in his enthusiasm at the idea of "peeking in" on it, not just once, but every 100 years!

In light of this unified experience of time, the artists' expressed lack of interest in their own past seems paradoxical.

Lack of Interest in a Time Other Than Their Own

An utterly unexpected response from the artists was the large share of disinterest they expressed in coming back after their death or visiting a period before their birth.[2] The reactions triggered off by this fantasy question are revealing. While the artists generally avoided asserting feelings of self-fulfillment when directly questioned about it, self-fulfillment did find expression on a visceral level when they were asked about any desire to return after death. In short, many artists expressed a lack of interest in anything more than this life. As Milstein put it, "It's all I want. It *fulfills* all my needs." And Stern quips, *"après moi le déluge,"* indicating that though he may not welcome death, he refuses to bargain for more than this life. Not wanting to come back at all, or choosing the 1,000-year interval, reflects an ability to let go of life, even a degree of death-acceptance—at least in fantasy.

---

[1] Only two of all other interviewees in the "over 30" age bracket mentioned experiencing time as a unity. The mathematician Ronald Graham is one of the two exceptions.

[2] All other people in that age group (N=120), with the exception of the physicist Eugene Wigner, would choose to come back.

If this analysis appears oversimplified, it becomes less so when we consider the explanations given by those who would choose to come back two years after their death.[3] The argument in favor of a speedy return included the desire to see family and friends and even one's own funeral. The question triggered frequent wish-fulfillment fantasies in the least self-actualized individuals; a common response involved the individual's interest in seeing how loved ones were reacting to her/his death. Occasionally, the interviewee wondered out loud if it was possible to be pronounced dead by mistake, insuring a quick return to life. Thus, at the opposite pole of the self-actualization dimension, the incompleteness of life manifests itself in the need to hang on to it, even after death—at least in fantasy.

Reluctance to Talk About Death

Also unexpected was the frequently encountered reluctance, if not downright aversion, to talk about death. It was again Milstein who put it most baldly: "What a shame to talk about death. . . . I would much rather discuss other things, such as life." Consistent with the disinclination to talk about death is the low conscious preoccupation with the topic, reflected in the responses to the question, "How often do you think about your own death?" One may wonder why people who are disinclined to think or talk about death agreed to the interview in the first place, knowing fully well its subject matter. Evidently, the feelings involved are highly ambivalent. Webster, for instance, seemingly ill at ease with the topic of death, is also intrigued by it. He admits to frequent thoughts about his impending death, and some time after the interview he even sent me his favorite aphorisms on death. On the other hand, Schneider, who seems most at ease with the prospect of eventual extinction, states that he does not think about it.

The artists' generally low preoccupation with death, in sharp contrast to the scientists' high preoccupation, may be rooted in their experience of death as an internal rather than an external force. These differences will be explored after all pertinent interviews have been presented.

---

[3] The two to ten year interval was the most frequent choice at every age bracket and at every level of accomplishment, with the exception of the artists and scientists.

The Role of Fame

There are indications that recognition and fame do play a part in the struggle to come to terms with death. Only when one possesses it—and in overabundance at that—does fame no longer seem important. Ashkenazy still remembers a time when fame was important, but it is no longer so. Now it does not even matter whether or not others appreciate his talents: "If you know that what you are doing is right, it doesn't matter when others recognize it; even if they never do." Almost the same feeling was expressed by Arkin: "I am only concerned with being good. . . . I do not have the need to be appreciated by thousands, now or later."

However, in Webster's case, where a name is a dictionary rather than a household word (his own pun), recognition is of utmost importance. Though Webster is very well-known and highly respected in the music world, he is relatively unknown outside of it. This is a fate he shares with many great pianists who do not rank among the two or three best known performers.[4] Interestingly, Webster could not pinpoint his ultimate goal, but he was unequivocal about the most unpleasant experience: "Not to be appreciated."

Fortunately, Beveridge Webster's greatest satisfaction seems to derive from the successes achieved by his own children and from his brilliant students. Since he is not indifferent to fame even after his death, it may be through them that he is carving out his own form of immortality.

Paul Doktor shares some of Webster's discontent; although he ranks among the very best violists in the music world, his name too is not a common household word. Doktor blames his relative obscurity on the viola, an instrument much less in demand and certainly not as recognized as the violin, which he once played equally well. He believes he would have been as well-known to the public as Heifetz, Stern, or Milstein had he remained a violinist.

Like Webster, not to be appreciated is the most unpleasant fate Doktor can think of. But he has not resigned himself to being anything less than world famous. His ultimate goal is still the same as it has

---

[4]In a survey conducted by one of my students, a majority of people, chosen at random, could not name more than two to four famous pianists.

always been: to be a musician of *reputation*. He feels that he has achieved that—but not completely. There seems to be room for only one world-famous viola player at a time. Only Primrose has occupied that place. And, with a twinkle in his eye, Doktor remarked that no one has replaced Primrose yet.

Of course, fame is not necessary (nor is it sufficient) to experience self-fulfillment. There are many highly self-actualized individuals who remain unknown to the public, and there are some very unfulfilled famous people. But fame does lend authenticity to our lives. It validates accomplishment of something uniquely our own, of having left a mark, of having had an impact on the world around us. Fame asserts existence itself.

Self-fulfillment and Readiness to Die

It is certainly evident that all of the artists interviewed here enjoy their profession immensely. They have led long and highly self-actualizing lives, with greater opportunities than most people to explore, develop, and use their talents. Yet even the most successful ones among them shun expressions of self-fulfillment. Thus, Stern most emphatically states that he has not yet achieved all he wants to achieve. Keenly aware of what he has not yet done and "still searching" for that all-elusive, ultimate goal, he certainly is not ready to die. He seems to be more impatient with death than afraid of it. He just has no time for it. Equating the fear of death with pre-performance nervousness is most revealing: he has learned to come to terms with both—to a point. He has not repressed his fears, admitting that "only a fool would not be nervous"; rather, he willfully *postpones* thinking about them, channeling his energy into more productive outlets. He is saying with Montaigne, "Why fear so long something so short?"

Milstein, though fifteen years older than Stern, rejects the idea of having reached self-fulfillment just as vehemently: he has not yet achieved all he wants or is able to do; "I don't feel I have reached the peak. . . . The important thing is that I am still changing." Clearly, he is not ready for death either. And in the same breath in which he tells us that he is not afraid of death, he talks about his fear of flying. This phobic reaction may very well serve as an effective defense against the unresolved conflict of having to die. The original fear is displaced to an avoidable object. As long as he does not fly he does not experience anxiety.

Ashkenazy puts it most bluntly: ". . . feeling fulfilled: No! That would be the end; I would be finished." Yet he tells us that he is ready to die any time and, indeed, he appears to be utterly at ease with himself and the world around him. Death does not seem to be a threat—perhaps because it is still so far off.

Both Paul Doktor and Alan Arkin, directly link readiness to die with self-fulfillment. While Doktor complains, "I am just not ready for it. I haven't accomplished all that I could accomplish," Arkin has no such apprehension: "Since I have done 'my thing' I am no longer afraid of death." Arkin's views of life and of death have been influenced by Eastern philosophy. Paradoxically, his ultimate goal can only be attained by "turning outward," though the resulting peak experience is an inner, very private state that cannot be expressed in words. It is as if one must lose oneself in order to find oneself. The claim that he has reached his limits, that he cannot surpass himself, makes one wonder if he has indeed actualized all his potentials and is now basking in a tension-free state that will last for the rest of his life. Or is this equanimity a temporary condition? Interestingly, Arkin and Ashkenazy, the two youngest artists I interviewed, were more at ease with the prospect of having to die than any of the others, with the possible exception of Alexander Schneider. Perhaps the accomplishment of so much so soon and the likelihood that a long time insulates them from death accounts for their greater equanimity.

One of the very few individuals who seems to have truly come to terms with death is Schneider. As far as his own life is concerned, it is completed; he has achieved his goals. But contrary to the general assumption that self-actualization is synonymous with happiness, Schneider does not impress one as a particularly happy man. A humanist, intensely concerned with the younger generations, he feels pessimistic about *their* future.

In a most unusual way, King too relates fulfillment to a readiness for death: "The most uncomfortable, the worst about having to die is to waste one's life." King's fears of death are religiously conditioned, as well as existential. The existential fear of death is expressed in the sentence quoted above, and it also comes out in his acute awareness of the limits of available time.

The complexity and contradictions arising from religiously conditioned fears are well illustrated here. On the one hand, there is denial of death: death is not final, but rather an improvement over the present condition, since " . . . one goes to another place that can only be better. . . ." Consistent with these teachings, he rates the concept "death" as highly positive on the semantic differential scale. On the other hand, he admits to being afraid of death, he fears the unknown, he only rarely thinks about death, and the confrontation with his mortality makes him feel uncomfortable.

In sharp contrast to King's apprehensions are Beall Smith's and Tobey's harmonious relationships with life and death. Though neither of them claims to have reached self-fulfillment, they do not refute it either. They do more than just confront and fully acknowledge their own mortality: they express appreciation for the positive aspects of death personified by Tobey as "the great motivator in all creative achievements." Since death is not viewed as a threat, the usual defenses of denial, repression, (phobic) displacement, or rationalization are absent. At times, Tobey would even welcome death, while Beall Smith is "fascinated" with it and emphasizes liking to think and to talk about death.

Of course, readiness to die is multidetermined, and although most artists linked it spontaneously to self-fulfillment, self-fulfillment is only one factor, albeit a most important one. Aside from deep-seated aspects of personality and of physical well-being, environmental and situational factors may also determine whether death is feared or welcome. There are no two people with identical attitudes toward death. Even similar responses occasionally conveyed different meanings. Nevertheless, the similarities in time- and death-orientation within the group of artists are remarkable.

But is it the artistic dimension or the level of self-actualization which is responsible for the homogeneous attitudes observed here? If it is the latter, then outstanding, creative scientists should share the artist's attitudes toward time and death. Indeed, Rosner and Abt (1970) found great similarities between creative artists and creative scientists in their reported experiences of the creative process, as well as in their general attitudes. Unfortunately, attitudes toward death were not explored in that study.

6

Interviews with Scientists

More light.

—*Goethe's last words*

In this chapter I am including two anonymous interviews. They are labeled Professor X and Professor Y. Both are prominent psychologists who did not want to be identified by name. Only the first two interviews will be followed immediately by discussions of them.

John A. Wheeler, Physicist

Biography

Born on July 9, 1911, in Jacksonville, Florida, Wheeler studied at Johns Hopkins University, where he earned a doctorate in 1933. He spent some time studying in Copenhagen with the renowned Danish physicist Niels Bohr with whom he would later develop the first general theory of nuclear fission in 1939.

For most of his career, Dr. Wheeler has taught at Princeton University (1938–1976) working with students who would later become distinguished in the field of physics by winning the Nobel Prize. During the war he designed plutonium production reactors for the Manhattan Project. And from 1950 to 1952 at the Los Alamos Scientific Laboratory he helped to design thermonuclear devices. At about the same time (1951–1953), Wheeler was chosen to head Princeton University's Project Matterhorn. He was also a member of the U.S. General Advisory Committee on Arms Control and Disarmament.

Among other distinguishing honors, Dr. Wheeler has received

the Enrico Fermi Award for his work in nuclear fission, the National Medal of Science, and the Albert Einstein Prize of the Strauss Foundation. He has been a Guggenheim Fellow and a Fulbright professor.

In 1976 he established the Center for Theoretical Physics and is currently teaching at the University of Texas at Austin.

John Wheeler is probably best known, however, for his work in gravitation physics and his study of massive, collapsed stars, which he named "black holes."

Interview

I.: What is your ultimate goal?

J.W.: To understand why we are here. The universe without any consciousness would not be the universe. We haven't found the meaning, but there must be one. These questions, about life and about death, are the most important to me. Not too long ago, I took six months' leave of absence, just to be able to talk to people who are also concerned with these questions—just trying to find some answers.

I.: How far would you be willing to go, or to sacrifice, to find some of the answers.

J.W.: There are no limits. I would do anything I can.

I.: If the only way to reach these levels of understanding demanded sacrificing part of your life, dying earlier—I am thinking of the kind of sacrifices some explorers or inventors have made—would you be willing to do that?

J.W. Yes, and even if it is not I, but others, who would have the answers.

I.: Which time perspective is the most important to you; past, present, or future?

J.W.: The future. I always plan projects ahead. My particular position is secondary. What's important are the problems, the projects, my work. As far as the past is concerned, I do keep record of past, I mean of my work; but only because it's like a mirror for the present.

I.: How long do you *expect* to live?

J.W.: To old age. Into the eighties.

I.: What is your preference, regarding time of death?

J.W.: The same. To reach old age.

I.: If after you died you could come back once for a short period, when would you choose to come back: 2, 10, 100, or 1,000 years after your death?

J.W.: It depends on what I would be able to do. If I can't contribute, then I may just choose to see my grandchildren. But if I can contribute, I would much rather come back in 1,000 years.

I.: If you could visit a past period, which one would you choose: two to ten years before your birth, around 1900, 1700 to 1900, antiquity, or any other?

J.W.: Around 1700.

I.: Why?

J.W.: I would have liked to be around when Leibniz was elected to the Academy of Sciences.

I.: If you created a masterpiece, what would you prefer: 1,000 readers now or 1,000 readers in 100 years?

J.W.: In 100 years. A present work is not important if it is no longer known 100 years from now.

I.: Are you afraid of death?

J.W.: I guess everybody is. That is probably what makes me think of it daily—and I mean daily, since I was ten years old and read about the deaths of World War I. I am also thinking about that biological push to stay alive. I had to drown kittens once, and I saw them push to stay alive. This biological push to stay alive is in me, and that's what makes me feel that I am afraid. But I also feel that life without death is meaningless. It's like a picture without a frame. Death gives value to life. More than that, without death there is no life.

Wheeler's overall semantic differential rating of the meaning of "death" was neutral, because of an equal amount of positive and negative qualities attributed to that concept. The negative attributes were: cruel, solitary, and dull; the positive ones were: fair, harmonious, and valuable. His evaluation of the meaning of "life" was highly positive.

Second Interview with John A. Wheeler

After reading the transcribed interview, Professor Wheeler felt that it did not go far enough in expressing his thoughts on death and he intended to elaborate on it.

Several years after the first interview, while Professor Wheeler was in New York as a participant of the Einstein Centennial Celebration, I had the occasion to conduct the second interview, presented below.

I.: Can you think of ever reaching a stage of complete fulfillment, of the actualization of all potentials, where there is no longer that push to stay alive, you had talked about before—no longer any fear of death?

J.W.: Let me answer in terms of the last days of my own father. He was still full of projects, ideas, and hopes. He still wrote letters to dozens and dozens of people, giving them encouragement in what they were doing. His spirit, his dreams for what needed to be done, continued as full as ever, but in the last two weeks his heart gave out and he felt physically just too tired to go on. His heart had been damaged when he was about thirty by scarlet fever and every year it was a miracle that he still survived.[1]

I.: In a way we all die prematurely. We have not achieved consistency between our physical and our mental longevity potentials.

J.W.: Einstein in his last days had a tired look. He gave me the feeling of someone who has given every last bit for his great cause.

I.: Was he "all there" mentally?

J.W.: Yes, indeed!

I.: Did he still have projects in view?

J.W.: He went to the hospital for the last days of his life and was still working, writing down his calculations up to the end.

I.: That's very interesting. Do you think that you have come to terms with death?

J.W.: In July 1977 after you had first interviewed me, I slipped on the wet grass and fell upside down over a cliff at the outlet of the famous Fiumi Latte near the shores of Lake Como in northern Italy. As I was falling and my head bounced from rock to rock, I felt the end had come; but strangely enough, I felt resigned to whatever was going to happen. However, if my airplane tomorrow night had to ditch in the ocean, I would struggle with all my might to survive. Life is just too precious to give up. In these later years, each remaining year seems more precious than ever; but even more, the contact with every friend

[1]Joseph Lewis Wheeler was distinguished librarian of Baltimore's Enoch Pratt Free Library.

enhances the preciousness of life. What a miracle it is to be able to communicate with someone who is really a human being, with hopes, ideas, and attitudes toward the world.

I.: I would like to push you a little harder on the question of being ready to die. Let us suppose in thirty years you have accomplished all you possibly could . . .

J.W.: In my office I keep a two-inch white box for every project that I plan to do someday. When I do the project and publish the paper, I bind up the working materials of that project for my records. The number of new projects that I add each year exceeds the number that I accomplish. So now there are about 150 such two-inch boxes in my office—misery for my poor secretary. To me each is a precious tie to the world. So it is hard for me to think of myself ever being tired of the world. You remember Dr. Samuel Johnson's words, "When a man is tired of London, he is tired of life." What he said about London applies to everything in my life.

I.: It looks like you won't run out of projects, you won't get tired of writing for the next 300 years. Do you think there is continued growth, continued creativity?

J.W.: The act of writing to me is not an act of reordering; it is an act of creation. But one's creativity depends so much on what others say and how others react! Creation to me is a magic consequence of one's interaction with those around.

I.: That's interesting, because it is in sharp contrast with the way a number of artists expressed themselves. They felt that their work is good, regardless of the opinion of others. Ashkenazy says that there is an absolute truth in art, independent of the reactions of others.

J.W.: To me science is not something written down on a piece of paper. It is a living, moving understanding that has its existence only in the mind of man. Science done, that does not enter the mind of man is not—to me— science. And growth is not purely internal matter; there is also growth in interaction with others.

I.: Some expect everything of science—even to be able, one day, to banish death. Would you banish death if you could?

J.W.: I shall come back to the importance of our expectations later; as for banishing death:
(1) Taking a responsibility for the trees at my children's summer place makes me aware of how a great old spreading tree kills the future for promising new young trees which are too close to it. Death is essential for renewal. We know that the world is renewed from underneath.

(2) Life without death would be a picture without a frame.

(3) To have the body go is proof before one's eyes that the survival of mankind, its essence, is of the spirit—the flame handed on from one runner to another. How else are we to realize that life is more important than the ones who do the living?

(4) The dream world of that fantastic play by J. P. Sartre, *Les jeux sont faits*, is enough to persuade one that all the preciousness and meaning of life would be drained away if one could go on living forever.

I.: The same point is made especially strongly in Giraudoux's *Amphitryon 38*.

J.W.: (5) We have many ways to judge people but none of more universal application than character in the face of death. I have known three survivors of Auschwitz—that most terrible place I ever visited in my life—two men and a woman. Never have I known anyone with more vitality, more love of life, than these three.

(6) Benedetto Croce tells us that if we are to understand anything, we should go back to its historical origins. The finiteness of life, we learn from Darwin and his followers, has evolved in such a way as best to ensure the continuation of life.

(7) I have at least a dozen books on death—from two on Auschwitz and one on Emily Dickinson to one called *The Private World of Dying Children*—from fascination with the idea that by understanding death better we will understand life better.

(8) We have no stronger way to mark our commitment to a great cause than to die for it. So long as there is any such thing as death, human beings can be great.

(9) Nobody can take away one's possibility to die for a cause. So long as that measure of ultimate commitment is attainable, the world will be a *live* place to live in. Were death to be abolished, all that we call precious in the world would die.

I.: What about our expectations of science eventually being able to abolish death?

J.W.: I don't think we will ever realize that expectation. However, in other areas of life, expectation is often the necessary precondition for achievement. That is nowhere more so in view than in the case of Einstein, and not only Einstein, but of others brought up in the Talmudic tradition. When by the age of thirteen a young man has proved himself excellent in Talmudic studies, he is relieved of some of his everyday burdens. In return, the young person not only has to go on excelling in his studies—or Einstein in his science—but he also has to take a responsibility for speaking up on the larger interests of the whole community.

Coming to terms with death
for the sake of life

In the struggle to reconcile himself with the necessity of his own death, Wheeler has focused on a way of coming to terms with death that I have neglected thus far: altruism—a rare concept in our "I, me, my" age.

His argument against banishing death, based primarily on ethical grounds, raises some intriguing questions. Though many of his points are well taken, he does seem, at times, to overstate the merits of death. Thus, one may question the importance of "character in the face of death." Is it important enough to keep death going, if we had the choice to do otherwise? For one thing, character does not change on the death bed. One faces death the same way one had faced other important events or crises throughout life. For another, how are we to judge character, even if it revealed itself most prominently in the face of death? Is it "better" to die like a Spartan—courageous, bold, defiant? Is it less noble to cling to life at all costs? Courage may stem from a lack of imagination, and cowardice from oversensitivity.

I also have some difficulty in accepting as positive attributes of death Wheeler's last two points which deal with the possibility of dying for a great cause. A stronger way to mark our commitment to a great cause may be to live for it, rather than to die for it. And the great cause of one may be the holocaust of another. If we could abolish the possibility of dying for a cause, we would abolish wars. Fanatics are the most likely to be willing to die for their "great cause"—I am not sure they have made the world a better place to live in. But then again, what kind of world would we be living in without the Curies, the Ghandis, the Pasteurs, the Galileos, and countless others, who were willing to die for the advancement of humanity?

Leaving all value judgments aside, having a cause one is ready to die for is certainly an effective way of coming to terms with death. It is a way of choosing death freely, instead of being its impotent victim. But it requires absolute conviction that the cause one is committed to is more important than one's life.

With Wheeler's perspective of the enormity of space and time, of billions of galaxies millions of light years apart, with all-devouring black holes swallowing worlds of matter, with time cut off at the gates of time—if one can fathom such a universe—one is, perhaps, able to transcend the anguish of one's own finiteness.

However, one can't say that Wheeler has resigned himself to accepting anything passively, without a struggle.[2] He has come to terms with death on one level and has not come to terms with it on another: he would not banish death, but neither can he conceive of ever being ready to die, of ever exhausting his potentials. (We have only to remember his 150 project boxes.) In his own words, "Life is just too precious to give up." It even becomes more precious with every remaining year! At the same time he *knows* that we *must* die for life to continue, and " . . . life is more important than the ones who do the living."

It has been noted elsewhere that Wheeler is fond of paradox. And, indeed, it is only when we go far enough to see that seemingly contradictory aspects can and do exist side by side that we can begin to understand the individual, the world, the universe. What Wheeler has said about the universe also applies to mankind: "Only when we recognize how strange the universe [man] is, will we understand how simple it [he] is."

Eugene Paul Wigner, Physicist

Biography

Eugene Paul Wigner has retired from teaching, but this 1963 Nobel Prize–winning physicist continues to lead an active professional life, involved in research projects at Princeton and Rockefeller University and as a guest lecturer. Born in Budapest, Hungary, in 1902, he studied chemical engineering and won a doctorate in engineering at the Technische Hochschule in Berlin. Throughout his life Dr. Wigner has collected a number of honorary degrees from prestigious universities throughout the world.

He taught physics at Princeton from 1930 to 1971 with interruptions. In 1936–1938 he taught at the University of Wisconsin, and in

---

[2]Freud remarked, "He who humbly resigns himself to the insignificant part man plays in the universe is . . . irreligious in the truest sense of the word" (*The Future of an Illusion*). Wheeler is certainly not irreligious in that sense.

1957 served as Lorentz lecturer at the Institute Lorentz in Leiden. Dr. Wigner was director of research and development at Clinton Laboratories in 1946–1947, and of the Civil Defense Research Project, Oak Ridge, Tennessee, in 1964–1965. He also served on the general advisory committee of the Atomic Energy Commission from 1952–1957.

In addition to the Nobel Prize, Dr. Wigner has received the Decorated Medal of Merit, 1946; the Enrico Fermi Award from the Atomic Energy Commission, 1958; the Atoms for Peace award, 1960; the Max Planck medal from the German Physical Society, 1961; and the National Science medal, 1969. And among his many memberships are the Royal Society of England; the Royal Netherlands Academy of Science and Letters; the American Nuclear Society (director, 1960–1961); the American Physical Society (vice-president, 1955; president, 1956); the American Philosophical Society; and the National Academy of Sciences.

Interview

E.P.W.: The highest goal worth reaching? To make my family happy. My true interest was not in fame or anything like that. I didn't truly desire all the honors that were given to me. But today I'm glad I got all the recognition I received, simply because it allowed me to do many things I wanted to do. It increased my influence in the outside world and made it easier for me to accomplish some of the things I felt should be done.

I.: Would you have been willing to make great sacrifices to do those things you wanted to do?

E.P.W.: If you mean doing a great deal of work, then one can't speak of sacrifices. Work is more like pleasure than anything else. I love my work. And you can't help your family by making sacrifices. One can't bring about happiness for others by work one does not like.

I.: In your experience of time, which dimension seems the most important: past, present, or future?

E.P.W.: I am future-oriented—and present, to a point. For instance, just sitting here with you and trying very hard to give correct answers, I am already looking forward to seeing something very exciting that is going on on the floor below, some scientific breakthrough someone just told me about. Even now, though I am interested in your questions, I am mostly oriented toward the future. The past is of lesser interest to me. I even forget events of the past.

I.: Are you keenly aware of time passing, of limits of available time?

E.P.W.: Not until very recently—somewhat more so, now.

I.: How long do you *expect* to live? Do you have any intuition about it?

E.P.W.: Yes, a relatively short time, perhaps ten years.

I.: Regardless of your expectations, what is your preference regarding time of death?

E.P.W.: Well, that depends. My wife has cancer. A few years ago, she was given only six months to live. But that did not come true. She's doing quite well. I fear the situation in which she will leave me here, but I also don't want to die before she does. I want to spare her that.

I.: You don't want to live after she dies, and you don't want to die before she does?

E.P.W.: No, for her sake I don't want to die first and often I fear the situation in which I won't have her any more.

I.: If after death you could come back once for a short period of time, when would you choose to come back: 2, 10, 100, or 1,000 years after death?

E.P.W.: (emphatically) Not at all!

I.: Why not?

E.P.W.: I am worried about what I would see. It could be sad.

I.: What about visiting a past period, before you were born. Which one would you choose?

E.P.W.: 1821—that's an interesting time to see.

I.: Would you prefer 1,000 people admiring your work now, or 1,000 people admiring it in 100 years?

E.P.W.: Doesn't make any difference. My prime interest was never in recognition, and I don't feel that my work is "important," I mean *vitally* important. I love the work. I am interested in it for its own sake, not because I believe it's important. I have initiated work on many subjects, both technical and purely scientific, but had I not done so, it would have been done by others. This actually applies, I believe, to all desirable human activities, even to the discovery of the theory of relativity. Einstein thought so.

I.: Are you afraid of death?

E.P.W.: I don't think so. It's very difficult to know, but I do not fear "not to exist." I have seen people who feared death. A great friend of mine, Von Neumann, did. He lost his mind when he knew he was going to die. No, I don't think I really fear the "nonexistence."

I.: How often do you think about your own death?

E.P.W.: Ten years ago I didn't truly believe in it. My emotions and most actions did not take the existence of death into account. Now I think about it, but I am not preoccupied with it. I think about it, for instance, when I file something. I wonder if I'll see it again.

Here is a man, a Nobel Prize recipient, who thinks of his accomplishments as of minor importance but struggles with the dilemma of having to outlive or being outlived by his spouse.

Wigner's interview was conducted at a time of personal crisis: his wife was dying. His apparent separation–abandonment fears have been expressed innumerable times by people who have spent most of their lives with a companion, even when there is no imminent death threat. Each dreads to outlive the other, but at the same time s/he wants to spare the other the grief of bereavement. Arnold Toynbee (1969) expressed the same sentiment: "If one truly loves one's spouse, one wishes her to die first, to spare her the sorrow of bereavement." In a large survey on attitudes toward death, Shneidman (1971) found that most people cannot make up their minds as to whether they wish to predecease or outlive their spouse. Those who had a preference divided equally between wanting and not wanting to outlive their mate.

Interestingly, responses to the question of "who should outlive whom" are often paradoxical and may depend on the wording of the question. Thus, when asked, "Do you want to outlive your mate?" a "yes" response is no assurance that the same person will reply "no" when asked, "Do you want your mate to outlive you?"

In these cases the focus is on survival—no matter whose. If the time of death of one spouse is more or less fixed (sickness, accident, old age, or just by the way the question is formulated), the desire is for the other one to survive. The question, "who would you prefer to die first, you or your mate?" can only be answered by "neither." Experiences, any experiences, even the most painful ones, are preferable to no experience at all.

The opposite paradox occurs just as frequently. Namely, this is the desire to die before one's companion does, and at the same time wishing for one's companion to die first.

This is the conflict Wigner expressed. The most pressing need here is to avoid the sorrow of bereavement, for oneself and for one's companion. The solution to this dilemma is frequently expressed by the wish to die together. Suicide pacts are often based on the need to spare each other this sorrow. Here too, the question, "Who would you prefer to die first?" cannot be answered, but for very different reasons than in the first case: the need to avoid suffering is stronger than the need for survival.

Neither egotism nor altruism play a major part in the conflicts outlined above. As a matter of fact, the dilemma stems from identifying with one's companion to a point where survival as well as grief by the other is experienced as one's own. Of course, many people do have a clear preference for either surviving or being survived by their mate.

Wigner's fears are fears of life rather than fears of death. By all indications he has come to terms with death. He has led a highly self-actualizing life; he has been able to do his thing, more than most, and he has loved it. However, the feeling of having done something vitally important, of having left a mark, of having accomplished something no one else could have done as well, is absent. On the contrary, he emphasizes that had he not discovered that atomic particle for which he was awarded the Nobel Prize, someone else would have done it in his place. The sentiment here is reminiscent of the one expressed by Wheeler: the importance of the individual lies in handing on the flame as one runner does to the other. The individual runner does not compete in *this* game.

Lyman Spitzer, Jr., Physicist

Biography

Dr. Spitzer was born in 1914. He has been teaching at Princeton since 1947, serving as Charles A. Young Professor of Astronomy (since 1952), chairman of his department, and director of the observatory. He directed its Project Matterhorn during 1953–1961, and in 1962—under the auspices of the National Aeronautics and Space Administration— he headed Princeton's program to design a telescope–spectrometer for an orbiting astronomical observatory. Since 1972, when *Copernicus* was launched, this Princeton telescope has been operating successfully.

From 1961–1966 he was primarily responsible for Princeton's Plasma Physics Lab, and in 1967 he was named to a five-year term as chairman of the University Research Board.

After receiving a bachelor's degree from Yale in 1935 and studying for a year at Cambridge University, he received his doctorate from Princeton in 1938. From 1939 until 1947 he was a member of the Yale faculty. In 1951 he developed an idea in controlled fusion research which led to the publication of his *Physics of Fully Ionized Gas.* He has continued to write scientific papers and books on stellar atmospheres, the origin of stars and of the solar system, interstellar matter, and controlled release of thermonuclear energy.

Spitzer is a recipient of the Rittenhouse medal, 1957; NASA's Exceptional Science Achievement medal, 1972, and Distinguished Service Medal, 1976; the Catherine Wolfe Bruce Gold medal, 1973; and the National Academy of Science Award of the Henry Draper medal, 1974. His many professional memberships include the American Academy of Arts and Sciences and the National Academy of Sciences. Dr. Spitzer also belongs to the Royal Society of Sciences of Liège and the Royal Astronomical Society, London.

Interview

I.: What is your ultimate goal in life?

L.S.: I have had two main concerns for the last thirty-five years: my work—its value, recognition, inner as well as external recognition, success. My main objectives are in the areas of its importance and elegance—architectural elegance. My second objective has been the happiness of my family. But this has become less of an objective, since my children are grown up it is less of my responsibility now.

I.: How far would you be willing to go, or to sacrifice, to reach the highest goal you consider worth reaching?

L.S.: Most of my pleasures are related to my work. I would have made important sacrifices, had this been necessary. But working is in itself no sacrifice. It's what I like best.

I.: In your subjective experience of time, which time dimension is the most important, past, present, or future?

L.S.: The future! One lives on one's hopes. I am always contemplating, always planning long in advance. There is also the long-range planning for academic years ahead, for future projects.

I.: Are you nostalgic about the past?

L.S.: No, not at all.

I.: How long do you *expect* to live?

L.S.: Another fifteen to twenty years.

I.: What is your preference, regarding time of death?

L.S.: To live as long as I am enjoying life. Not just to be alive. It must have value.

I.: If after you died you could come back once for a short period, when would you choose to come back: 2, 10, 100, or 1,000 years after your death?

L.S.: Certainly not two or ten years. That is not long enough for important changes to have occurred; there would be no information of any intellectual interest. A thousand years would be of the greatest intellectual interest. I have a mild preference for 1,000 years since in addition this would be less emotionally distressing than 100 years.

I.: If you could visit a past period, which one would you choose: two to ten years before your birth, around 1900, 1700 to 1900, antiquity, or any other?

L.S.: Antiquity. Time of the Greek or Roman empire. Just out of curiosity. To get a more accurate picture. The Renaissance would also be interesting.

I.: If you created a masterpiece, what would you prefer: 1,000 readers now or in 100 years?

L.S.: Doesn't matter very much. Now is somewhat more attractive.

I.: Are you afraid of death?

L.S.: No. Not intellectually. Naturally, if one has done what one has been equipped to do, one can die. Eternal life would be a disaster.

I.: How often do you think about your own death: daily, once a week, once a month, hardly ever?

L.S.: Perhaps as often as once a month.

On the semantic differential rating scale, his overall rating of the meaning "death" was slightly negative, while his overall rating of "life" was positive.

Ira B. Bernstein, Physicist

Biography

Ira Bernstein is New York born and educated. He received his bachelor of chemical engineering from the City University of New York in 1944 and his doctorate in theoretical physics from New York University in 1950. From 1948 to 1950 he was Research Fellow at the Brookhaven National Laboratory in Upton, New York. From 1950 to 1954 he was Research Physicist at the Westinghouse Research Laboratory in East Pittsburgh, Pennsylvania. In 1954 he was appointed Research Associate at Princeton University until 1962, when he received the appointment of Senior Research Physicist at Princeton until 1964. During 1962–1963 Dr. Bernstein was the Fulbright Senior Research Fellow at the Laboratorio Gas Ionizzati in Frascati, Italy.

In 1964 Ira Bernstein became professor at the department of engineering and applied science at Yale University. Since 1971 he has been Director of Graduate Studies at the department.

In 1969 Dr. Bernstein was Visiting Professor and Guggenheim Fellow of the Imperial College in London; and in the spring term of 1973 he was Visiting Member at the Institute for Advanced Study at Princeton.

Dr. Bernstein served as a consultant in Plasma Physics at RCA in Princeton, New Jersey, 1960–1964, and at the Princeton Plasma Physics Lab, at Princeton University, 1964. Since 1966 he has been a consultant to the United Aircraft Research Lab; since 1967 to the Los Alamos Scientific Lab; since 1971 to Lawrence Livermore Lab; and since 1973 to the Naval Research Lab.

Interview

I.: What do you conceive as your ultimate goal?

I.B.: I don't have a well-formulated goal. I never thought it through very carefully. I would like to have some professional accomplishments, a sense that I produced some good students and a decent family life. But there is no overwhelming single goal.

I.: Do you feel you have essentially achieved what you wanted to achieve?

I.B.: Well, one always wishes to improve things. I have the feeling of many more things to do and I don't see any end to continuing the same kind of life I am currently engaged in.

I.: How important is the idea of pushing knowledge ahead?

I.B.: That's a rather abstract thing. I think subjectively it is perhaps a more dominant sense of game-playing—I enjoy the work. It's probably the same kind of satisfaction that a chess player gets at winning the game. The notion of social service—of pushing knowledge forward is a little more abstract.

I.: It's more like problem solving?

I.B.: Yes. I enjoy problem solving. No grandiose scheme. I enjoy interacting with people who have the same interests. There is a pleasure perhaps in doing something that may be socially useful—but the real human satisfaction is that of a game player.

I.: If you were to come across a stage where you had to work day and night—abstaining from doing things you like to do—such as traveling . . .

I.B.: Of course I would! One goes into something like a creative frenzy—when one functions well one is likely to forgo anything else.

I.: You would be willing to sacrifice . . .

I.B.: It wouldn't be a sacrifice for me. Perhaps it would be for those around me.

I.: What is your most dominant time perspective: past, present, or future?

I.B.: I live only in the present.

I.: Any nostalgia about the past—ever wishing you could bring it back?

I.B.: I don't spend much time doing that. I sometimes look at periods of my life which I felt were professionally most fruitful. But one can't go back.

I.: How about projecting into the future?

I.B.: I find that very difficult too. I have a sense of lack of control over the future. It always seems to be the intervention of the unanticipated, or of the forces that I cannot influence.

I.: What about daydreams—do they involve past happenings or rather future anticipation?

I.B.: Oh, they are more future-oriented. They're "future fantasies."

I.: How long do you *expect* to live?

I.B.: Well, judging by my parents and grandparents, I might very well live to be ninety-four. I come from very long-lived families.

I.: How long would you *prefer* to live?

I.B.: If I could go on functioning well into old age, that would be fine. But what frightens me is what I see happening with my father. He is now ninety-five years old and senile. I find that very, very frightening. He does not enjoy life. He was a very bright, vigorous man and now he is a dottering old man. The important thing is to function well.

I.: If you could come back after you died, just for a short visit, but you would have to decide now when to come back, would you choose 2, 10, 100, or 1,000 years after your death?

I.B.: Probably 100. Things might be too bad after 1,000.

I.: That's funny. A few people said exactly the opposite. They would choose 1,000 years because things might be bad in 100.

I.B.: That shows you who the optimist is.

I.: What do you mean?

I.B.: I just think that things are becoming progressively more difficult for human beings.

I.: If you could visit a period in the past would you choose ten to twenty years before your birth, 1900, 1700 to 1900, antiquity, or any other?

I.B.: I would be tempted to choose antiquity. It always seems more romantic—Greece or Rome at its height.

I.: Are you afraid of death?

I.B.: Yes. Not terrified. I view death as oblivion. But since I don't believe in a hell or a heaven, it's not really a great fear. "Sad" is perhaps more correct. I don't know how to put it.

I.: Regrets?

I.B.: Yes! "Regrets" is a better description of the way I feel about it.

I.: How often do you think of death: daily, once a week, once a month, hardly ever?

I.B.: Once a week, when I visit my father.

I.: I mean, think about your own death.

I.B.: Yes, but it follows from seeing my father. It suddenly becomes reality.

I.: If you could have chosen a period in which to live your life, would you have chosen your own period, a period in the past, or in the future?

I.B.: Probably my own period. I have a feeling that it has been a period of maximum opportunity.

I.: If we found a way of banishing death would you be in favor of it? Would you make a contribution to achieve this end?

I.B.: Leaving the person in what kind of condition?

I.: As a well-functioning adult.

I.B.: As a mature adult, functioning well, professionally, without deterioration—sure!

I.: You would banish death?

I.B.: For myself, yes.

I.: For mankind? I mean, we would truly abolish death.

I.B.: Then you would have to abolish birth simultaneously.

I.: Yes, with all of the consequences you can think of.

I.B.: Probably selfishly, yes. Since I have a distaste for oblivion.

I.: Even if you really think it through—with all its obvious consequences?

I.B.: As an individual, if the choice left me free of decay, without all the usual unpleasant consequences we now endure—clearly I would welcome it.

I.: You don't think you would get bored to death? Well, you couldn't, if there is no death.

I.B.: No. There are certainly enough things in life to turn one's attention to.

I.: For millions of years?

I.B.: Yes.

I.: You have no doubts that one could go on and on being interested in it all?

I.B.: No doubts, it could go on. That is one of the fine things of intellectual activity; it's inexhaustible.

I.: You don't think that we have a given amount of potential that could eventually be used up?

I.B.: I think essentially the universe is infinite as to the things that could be known.

I.: And the mental potential is also infinite?

I.B.: The mental potential with regard to artistic creativity, scientific creativity, I think is bottomless.

I.: Thus, if you lived for another 300 years, you would not exhaust your potentials?

I.B.: That's correct. If you give me the condition that one doesn't stultify, I feel that most able people have the capacity for continued intellectual growth. People can continue to be intellectually creative, to learn and take pleasure in it. Indeed, with regard to creativity, apart from a few acts of geniuses, the person who is extremely able can become more so as time goes on, through the accumulation of experience.

I.: In that case we could never reach self-fulfillment. Can you think of ever experiencing fulfillment, of ever feeling, "I have done it all."?

I.B.: No. I don't conceive of life in terms of well-defined goals so that once I have achieved them, I am through. It's an ongoing thing. And interests and opportunities change. It's more important to be able to function and interact with others and get pleasure out of what you do. The only frightening thing is the loss of faculties.

I.: Is there anything more important than your life? Do you believe you could sacrifice it for anything?

I.B.: Yes, for the traditional things like defense of family or protecting the way of life one believes in.

I.: You mean for your ideology?

I.B.: Yes, I could feel strongly enough about it to risk my life. For instance, the Second World War; there was no question about putting your life on the line, in contrast to the Vietnam War, when one rather goes to Canada.

On the semantic differential rating scale, Ira Bernstein evaluated both "life" and "death" as slightly negative.

Henry Margenau, Physicist

Biography

Born in Bielefeld, Germany, in 1901, Henry Margenau received his Ph.D. degree from Yale in 1929. After 41 years on the Yale faculty, Dr. Margenau retired in 1969 as Eugene Higgins Professor of Physics and

Natural Philosophy, Emeritus. He has since been active with his research work and lectures around the country.

During World War II he worked on microwave theory, and his theory of spectral-line broadcasting was used in analyzing the fireball of the first hydrogen bomb. Professor Margenau has also served as a consultant to the Atomic Energy Commission, the Air Force, the National Bureau of Standards, the Argonne National Laboratory, the Rand Corporation, General Electric, and Lockheed and Avco Research Laboratories.

Henry Margenau has been the recipient of a Guggenheim Fellowship and a Fulbright Grant and has published over 200 scientific and philosophical articles. His books have been translated into numerous languages, including Japanese and Arabic. A book in his honor, entitled *Vistas in Physical Reality*, appeared in 1975.

A past president of the Philosophy of Science Association and a member of the most prestigious academies and societies, Professor Margenau also served as Associate Editor of *The American Journal of Science; The Review of Modern Physics; The Journal of Chemical Physics; Philosophy of Science; International Journal of Theoretical Physics; Foundations of Physics;* and *Main Currents.* He has been distinguished visiting professor at universities throughout this country as well as the universities of Tokyo (Japan) and of Fribourg (Switzerland), and twice Visiting Professor at Heidelberg (Germany). In 1957 and 1959 he was appointed National Visiting Scholar by Phi Beta Kappa.

In 1955, Dr. Margenau received the Michigan State University's Centennial Award for his work in physics and philosophy, and in 1969 the DeVane Medal of Yale's Phi Beta Kappa chapter.

Interview

H.M.: My ultimate goal? To feel that I have made some contribution to science and philosophy; to feel that I have resolved some current problems.

I.: How much would you sacrifice to achieve that goal?

H.M.: As far as I am concerned, it is not a question of sacrifices. I am retired now. I am Professor Emeritus—but I work just as hard as I ever did. That is what I *want* to do. But I do not want to sacrifice the well-being of others, especially of my wife.

I.: What is your dominant time orientation? Do you focus most on the past, the present, or the future?

H.M.: I can answer this only in terms of my work: during the last year I was very much interested in the past, because I had to bring up to date a book for publication, which is based on my work in philosophy and physics. But at present all my attention, all my effort, is devoted to resolving difficulties on philosophical issues; thus I am primarily preoccupied with what lies ahead, with what I am going to do.

I.: With the future?

H.M.: Yes, that's correct.

I.: How about a less professional, more "private" perspective? Are you nostalgic about the past? Do you dwell a great deal on the past?

H.M.: No, not at all! Though I had a very pleasant and memorable past. But I certainly don't dwell on it.

I.: How long do you *expect* to live?

H.M: I have no intuitions whatsoever. But I have no reason to believe that death is very imminent. I am just as vigorous as ever, though there are some physical discomforts. My expectations are perfectly normal for my age. Now, what I plan to do during the years left to me, is the following: My past was devoted to two kinds of problems: theoretical physics, which involves a great deal of elaborate mathematics, and the philosophy of science, specifically epistemology. For the future I will have to forgo the analysis of specific mathematical problems. As we grow older our analytic ability lessens; however, our general view of the world and of life is not impaired. Therefore I want to use what time may be left for me, resolving certain philosophical problems that have plagued me for many, many years.

I.: Do you have any preference as to the time of your death?

H.M.: No, I really don't. I am resigned to whatever fate holds in store for me. My only concern is the welfare of my family—my children and my wife, who is much younger than I am.

I.: Would you prefer to outlive her or to die before she does?

H.M.: I have no preference. But since she is ten years younger than I, I hope that she will survive me.

I.: If after you died you could come back once for a short period of time, when would you choose to come back: 2, 10, 100, or 1,000 years after your death?

H.M.: Well, I am really not very curious. I have lost my curiosity because

I am rather pessimistic about the future. I guess I would choose twenty years because it would still be somewhat connected with things that are going on. I would be able to see what happened to the people I love. The world would not be entirely estranged.

I.: If you could visit a period in the past would you choose two to ten years before your birth, 1700 to 1900, antiquity, or any other period?

H.M.: I find this question a little difficult to answer—it has never occurred to me. I think I would choose classical antiquity. The ages of the Greeks or the Roman Empire, perhaps. This choice is partially conditioned by the great interest I had in classical literature. I majored in Latin and studied the Ancients with great care.

I.: Are you afraid of death?

H.M.: No.

I.: Can you explain that? I mean, most people fear death—how come you don't?

H.M.: The only possible fear I may have is of dying painfully.

I.: No, I don't mean fear of dying, but fear of death—of no longer existing.

H.M.: And you ask why I do not have any apprehensions? Well, the various possibilities as to sequels of bodily death are not especially frightening to me. If it means complete extinction there is no suffering whatsoever. And the other possibilities I have thought about a great deal and more or less accepted bear no threat.

I.: What other possibilities? Are you thinking of a mind–body dichotomy and a possible continuation . . .

H.M.: Yes, yes! I am not sure if after death one has any reminiscences of the present life or whether the past is completely extinguished. I cannot say.

I.: If you did know that there will be no experiences—would complete extinction be a threat?

H.M.: No. I have done what I was able to do. I also received the recognition that one can expect from the sort of career I pursued. I have no regrets as to the content of my life. There is nothing there that worries me. I have reached my goals.

I.: How often do you think of your own death?

H.M.: At my age one thinks of death. One thinks of the arrangements that have to be made for the comfort of one's family; one thinks of making a will. That's about it. I think about it, but not daily.

I.: Is death an external force or an internal force?

H.M.: I would say internal.

I.: Would you favor banishing death if science were capable of doing that?

H.M.: No. I think it would be terribly boring to live forever. Of course if one could go on living with increased capacity for research, for knowledge, for growth—perhaps that would be different. That's not likely to be the case. In my philosophy, a finite life is the desirable thing. I would not wish to live forever.

I.: If we could extend our life span to its full potential—perhaps to 130 years—do you think we would exhaust our mental potentials as well as our physical ones?

H.M.: Yes, if life is as we now know it, I think one would use up one's potentials.

I.: Is it easier to die if one has actualized one's potentials?

H.M.: Oh, yes! Yes! The problems I am working on now are so difficult, they certainly can't be solved in one lifetime. The best expectation I have is to be able to make a dent. I want to produce some material that will lead to a new outlook on the set of problems I have chosen. I am working on the science of consciousness. We do not have a science of consciousness. Mental states are not translatable into numbers that can be handled by the usual mathematical processes. Thus, we are dealing with a field in which qualitative judgment must predominate. It has never been fully recognized that we need a wholly new approach to the problem of consciousness, to the problem of life and to the problem of death. I have come to the conclusion that the customary assertions of neo-Darwinism, namely random mutation and survival of the fittest, is not sufficient to explain the evolutionary process. We cannot understand evolution without invocation of purpose.

I.: You mean we need a teleological principle?

H.M.: Yes. And I have found that this agrees largely with the views of some very eminent biologists and neurophysiologists. I don't think one can understand evolution without injecting purpose, that is to say, teleology, in some form.

Returning to his work on a science of consciousness, Margenau spoke of the necessity to postulate a cosmic consciousness to be able to account for the phenomenon of the universe as we behold it.

Ronald L. Graham, Mathematician

Biography

Ronald L. Graham received his bachelor's degree in physics from the University of Alaska in 1958. From 1959 to 1962 he studied and took his master's and doctorate in mathematics from the University of California. In 1960 Graham also received a NSF Graduate Fellowship, and in 1961 a Woodrow Wilson Graduate Fellowship.

Since 1962 Graham has been employed by Bell Laboratories as head of their Discrete Mathematics Department. Presently, his work involves combinatorics (in 1972 he won the Polya Prize for Combinatorics), number theory, algorithms, and application of these disciplines to real-life problems.

In 1975 Dr Graham also served at UCLA as the Regent's Professor of Mathematics.

Interview

R.G.: What I want most out of my life—my ultimate goal? Pushing ahead in mathematics and other areas, being creative, exploring the unknown.

I.: How far would you be willing to go, or to sacrifice, to achieve what you want to achieve?

R.G.: There are no limits. Whatever you really want, you must want it irrationally. For instance, I want to learn Chinese. When the time comes, I will study ten hours a day if necessary. If you seriously want to accomplish something, you can't set any limits on the effort you are willing to put into it.

I.: In your subjective experience of time, which time dimension is the most important: past, present, or future?

R.G.: All of it. There is no sharp differentiation—they are one. I think about the past, I stay in touch with old friends, I listen to old records. I remember the better things of the past and enjoy them in the present. I enjoy and participate actively in the present. But in a way, you always live right in the future. In order to bring about the future you want, you must plan for it now. I plan to learn to juggle seven balls, which means that I have to practice for hundreds of hours in the present to be able to do it in the future. The important point is that one must plan for the present we want to have.

I.: What you are saying is that what we call the future now becomes the present. You are working now for a time in your life when you will know Chinese. Once we have realized or actualized a potential, it is no longer a *future* expectation, but part of our *present* experience.

R.G.: Yes, that's right, as far as it goes. But in my experience there is much less of a distinction between these dimensions.

I.: How long do you expect to live?

R.G.: I expect to live into old age. That's a change. When I was twenty, I didn't think I would make it to thirty.

I.: What is your preference regarding time of death?

R.G.: The later the better. I like life, whatever if offers.

I.: If after you died you could come back once for a short period, when would you choose to come back: 2, 10, 100, or 1,000 years after your death?

R.G.: A thousand years! So much is going to happen—in mathematics, in science.

I.: If you could visit a past period, which one would you choose: two to ten years before your birth, 1900, 1700 to 1900, antiquity, or any other?

R.G.: As far back as one can go. The creation of the universe. A time we know least about.

I.: If you created a masterpiece, a great discovery, would you prefer to have 1,000 readers now, or in 100 years?

R.G.: I guess I would choose now, but it's not particularly important to me.

I.: Are you afraid of death?

R.G.: No. I don't think so. I feel that if you play your cards right, one life is enough. I mean that if one has lived, one can die.

I.: How often do you think about your own death?

R.G.: Very rarely. I am not preoccupied with it. I have no life insurance, I have not made a will, I have not donated my body. It's not important to me.

I.: Would you sacrifice your life for anything? For instance a cause, a person?

R.G.: I don't think so, but one never knows how one would react. If someone were threatening my son with a gun, I would probably protect him. But that doesn't mean anything, because you never think that you are really going to die. You, yourself, are always "indestructible." As in war, it is everybody else who gets shot, not you. Otherwise no one would ever make a move forward.

I.: If you knew you had only one year to live, would you make any changes in your life-style?

R.G.: I would want to have the most important things yet undone finished by the time I leave.

On the semantic differential rating scale, Graham evaluated the meaning of death slightly negatively and the meaning of life highly positively.

Herman A. Witkin,[3] Psychologist

Biography

Born in New York in 1916, Professor Witkin received his bachelor's degree as well as his master's and doctoral degrees from New York University in 1935. While a graduate student, he worked with T. C. Schneirla on the study of animal behavior. From 1940 to 1952, while teaching at Brooklyn College, he did research in space orientation and individual differences. Obtaining a National Research Council Fellowship for 1943–1945, he worked with Max Wertheimer and Wolfgang Köhler. Witkin dates the beginning of his lifelong interest in cognitive styles to this period.

In 1952 he was appointed professor in the department of psychiatry at the SUNY Downstate Medical Center. Since 1971 Professor Witkin has continued his research in the Division of Psychological Studies of the Educational Testing Service in Princeton as their Senior Research Psychologist and chairman of the Personality and Social Behavior Research Group.

---

[3]While preparing this manuscript for publication I learned of Professor Witkin's death. *The New York Times* obituary noted Dr. Witkin's international status as a psychologist. It also mentioned that he was listed by the Institute for Scientific Information as among the 100 authors most frequently mentioned by the Social Sciences Citation Index. Others similarly listed are John Dewey, Sigmund Freud, and Margaret Mead.

In 1977 Queen Juliana of the Netherlands awarded Professor Witkin an honorary doctorate of social sciences from Tilburg University. And in 1979 he received the Research Review Award presented by the American Educational Research Association. He is also Honorary Fellow of the International Association of Cross Cultural Psychology.

Interview

H.W.: I really cannot talk about an ultimate goal. I am satisfied with the things I have done and with what I am doing now. I like my life. If you ask what's most important to me, it's the happiness of my family.

I.: If you had to make choices, had to sacrifice some parts of your present way of living, to continue doing things that are most important to you, what would you be willing to give up?

H.W.: I would give up anything rather than the life I am leading with my wife. You know, we were a "liberated couple" long before it became fashionable. My wife is a scientist, and there was a time, at the beginning of our careers, when she went to work and I took care of our home.

I.: Which time dimension is most important to you, subjectively: past, present, or future?

H.W.: I am not interested in the past. I am very present-oriented, but I am also planning actively for the future: the place we want to live when we retire, my future activities, etcetera.

I.: Are you overwhelmingly aware of time passing, of the limits of available time?

H.W.: The "not enough time" is chronic. I am not overwhelmingly tense about it, but I never have enough time. I am always doing too many things, and I am aware that I should cut down, but I can't.

I.: How long do you *expect* to live?

H.W.: To old age.

I.: What is your *preference* regarding time of death?

H.W.: Oh, about the same.

I.: Old age? The later the better?

H.W.: Yes, the later the better.

I.: If after you died you could come back once for a short period, when would you choose to come back: 2, 10, 100, or 1,000 years after your death?

H.W.: In a way 1,000 years would be most interesting. But more important would be to see how people who matter to me are faring. That's more like ten years after my death.

I.: If you could visit a past period, which one would you choose: two to ten years before your birth, around 1900, 1700 to 1900, antiquity, or any other?

H.W.: 1700 to 1900. Because of the quality of life. I am thinking of this country. It was a time of "decency."

I.: If you created a masterpiece, would you prefer 1,000 readers now, or in 100 years?

H.W.: Now.

I.: Are you afraid of death?

H.W.: No. I don't want to die, but I have fulfilled myself. I have no fear.

I.: How often do you think about your own death: daily, once a week, once a month, hardly ever?

H.W.: There is a difference in how it is initiated; inner-initiated, perhaps once a month—outer-initiated at least once a week.

I.: Do you think you would sacrifice your life for any of the following: a great cause, scientific advancement, a person?

H.W.: For a cause, yes. For scientific advancement, no! Certainly for my wife and children, but also for others who are in desperate need of help, even if I knew that I was risking my own life.

I.: If you knew you had only one year to live, would you make any changes in your life-style? Satisfy hedonistic needs, become more altruistic, or others?

H.W.: No, I would make no changes.

I.: How did this interview make you feel? Anxious? Apprehensive? Bored with the topic?

H.W.: Not at all. I liked it. I *love* life, but I am fully aware of death, and I feel no apprehension.

On the semantic differential rating scale, Witkin evaluated the meaning of "death" somewhat negatively, and the meaning of "life" positively.

Professor X, Psychologist

Biography

Professor X has been on the faculty of one of our most prestigious universities for almost twenty years. He has been a Guggenheim and a Fulbright fellow, and he is also the recipient of a number of distinguished awards. Professor X was born in the eastern United States in the early 1920s.

Interview

X: The highest goal I would like to achieve? Peace and tranquility! Of course I am being partly facetious. It's because of my present family situation, which is all but peaceful. I guess my work *is* the most important thing in my life. I would not sacrifice it for anything.

I.: Which is your most dominant time dimension: past, present, or future?

X: Oh, I am definitely future-oriented. As far as the present is concerned, I am constantly aware that I do not have enough time.

I.: How long do you expect to live?

X: A relatively short time; somewhere between fifteen and twenty years.

I.: How long would you want to live, if you had a choice?

X: To a ripe old age. Just short of senility.

I.: If you could come back once after you died, when would you choose to come back: 2, 10, 100, or 1,000 years after your death?

X: A hundred years. To see what happened at a time I can still relate to.

I.: If you could visit a period in the past, which one would you choose: two to ten years before your birth, 1900, 1700 to 1900, antiquity, or any other?

X: Antiquity. I have a passion for ancient Greece.

I.: If you created a masterpiece in art or made a great scientific discovery, would you prefer 1,000 people admiring your work now, or in 100 years?

X: Absolutely now! I don't care about immortality.

I.: Are you afraid of death?

X: Yes. I don't know why I said that. I am really not [afraid]. If you asked if I am acutely aware of it, yes! I am also keenly disappointed that one has to die. And I am uncomfortable on airplanes. But I think that has to do with having a very young son. But these regrets are not fear of death. I do not *fear* it—I am not anxious—but I don't like it.

I.: How often do you think about your own death?

X: Daily. I also read the obituaries daily. Or at least there are periods when I read them. It's kind of reassuring—you don't find your own name—you are still alive.

I.: Do you think you would sacrifice your own life for anyone or anything?

X: I think so. Not for a cause but perhaps for a person. I think I would for my son.

I: Would you make any changes in your life-style if you knew you had only one year to live?

X: Yes. I would satisfy my hedonistic needs.

On the semantic differential rating scale, his overall ratings of "death" as well as of "life" were slightly negative.

Asked about his reaction to the interview, he expressed disappointment: "You mean that's all you want to know of me? I would have liked it to go on and to go deeper. I like to think about death and to talk about it. Tell me more about the study."

He agreed with the major hypotheses and after looking at the list of interviewees he added, "I am glad that these people were willing to talk about death. I think you should also interview trumpet players."

I.: Why trumpet players?

X: I am sure there is a relation between the choice of a wind instrument and a person's attitude toward death. The most critical survival mechanisms, air and breathing, are chosen here as the medium for creativity. This could be an important dimension in your investigation. If you weren't such a snob [based on my remark that I was presently interviewing only highly accomplished artists and scientists] I may have gotten you interviews with some great jazz trumpet players.

At the end he not only refused me an introduction to trumpet players, but he also objected to being identified here.

Professor Y, Psychologist

Biography

Ever since Professor Y received his Ph.D. from the University of California, about 30 years ago, he has been on the faculty of two Ivy League Universities. Professor Y is a past president of a major psychological organization.

Interview

I.: What do you conceive as the height of fulfillment, your ultimate goal?

Y: Doing things well by my criteria.

I.: Would you be willing to make great sacrifices to accomplish that?

Y: There are no sacrifices; this is the only way to live.

I.: In your own experience of time, which is your most important time dimension: past, present, or future?

Y: The future. Future plans, in general.

I.: How long do you expect to live?

Y: A relatively short time.

I.: What is your preference regarding time of death?

Y: This is an irrelevant question. I don't have the choice.

I.: If after you died you could come back once for a short period of time, when would you choose to come back: 2, 10, 100, or 1,000 years after your death?

Y: A thousand years.

I.: Why?

Y: Curiosity. That is the longest perspective.

I.: If you could visit a past period, which one would you choose: two to ten years before your birth, 1900, 1700 to 1900, antiquity, or any other?

Y: Antiquity. For the same reason as I chose 1,000 years after my death.

I.: If you create a masterpiece, would you prefer 1,000 readers now or in 100 years?

Y: In 100 years, because that means it has value.

I.: Are you afraid of death?

Y: No. I have good defense mechanisms.

I.: How often do you think about your own death: once a week, once a month, hardly ever?

Y: More than once a week, perhaps daily. Living in "Big City" with children, you are forced to think about it. Questions of private or public school, insurance policies, all these decisions are influenced by an awareness of death. But I don't like to think about death, particularly at this period of my life. It would be a disaster for my family.

On the semantic differential rating scale, he rated the meaning of death as slightly negative and the meaning of "life" as positive.

Howard Gruber, Psychologist

Biography

Born in New York in 1922, Professor Gruber received his Ph.D. from Cornell in 1950. He had teaching appointments at Queen's College in Canada and at the University of Colorado, where he held the position of associate professor until 1963. Concurrently he held a visiting lectureship at University College, London (1955), and a visiting professorship at Cornell (1962–1965). In 1963 Dr. Gruber was appointed professor and chairman of the graduate psychology department at the New School for Social Research. In 1966 he cofounded the Institute of Cognitive Studies at Rutgers University, where he holds the position of professor of psychology. Concurrently he served as Research Associate of Harvard University (1966–1968).

Howard Gruber's areas of interest include experimental, developmental, and educational psychology; creativity; perception; thinking; and the history of science. Most of these interests found expression in his recently published monumental book *Darwin on Man*, of which Jean Piaget, who wrote the foreword, remarked:

> This fine work on the thought of Charles Darwin is an instructive and stimulating example of what the approach of genetic epistemology can produce when applied to the development of the theories of a great scientist. . . . the present work carries an evident epistemological

significance, making us understand how much a new scientific theory differs from a simple "reading" or description of the observed or observable facts. . . .

In a word this remarkable work is of high interest and we must hail it and be thankful for its original approach to this domain, in general so poorly explained, of scientific creativity.

Interview

I.: What do you want out of life? What do you conceive as the height of fulfillment?

H.G.: Achieving a better society. Developing an image of man which will work to better man. This is what I work for in my creativity studies.

I.: How much of yourself would you be willing to sacrifice to attain that goal?

H.G.: It's not a sacrifice, it's my pleasure.

I.: Thinking about it in very concrete terms, would you say that you would be willing to endure complete abstinence of everything that may interfere with or distract from your goal? Going even a step further, would you sacrifice part of your life, I mean, die earlier, for the sake of achieving your goal?

H.G.: Ten years ago I would not have hesitated to say, yes, I would die for what I believe in, or for what I wanted to do. It's not that I value my life more now, than I did then—but I don't see now how any of that can have any effect. My "sacrifices" cannot have any effect on what I would like to bring about.

I.: What is your most important time dimension? Do you live primarily in the past, the present, or the future?

H.G.: Definitely not the past! Intensely in the present, and there is a great deal of involvement in the future. On two levels: Realistically, I do a fair amount of planning and on a fantasy level it's about solving social problems.

I.: Are you overwhelmingly aware of time passing, of the limits of available time?

H.G.: Overwhelmingly, no. I am not tense about it, but I am aware of it. From time to time I try to save time.

I.: How long do you expect to live?

H.G.: Realistically, sixty-five to seventy years. I am basing that prediction on Fermi's principle: best estimate of tomorrow's high temperature is today's high temperature. My father died at sixty-five. But I am an optimist; I think I will have a few more years.

I.: What is your preference, regarding time of death?

H.G.: The later the better.

I.: If after you died you could come back once for a short period, when would you choose to come back: 2, 10, 100, or 1,000 years after your death?

H.G.: A thousand years. In two or ten years nothing much will have changed. A 100 years from now may very well be a very bad time. The aftermath of a great upheaval, whatever form that may take, or the very beginning of a new order. That's always a very tough time. In 1,000 years one could have great perspective, see the most of what has, or what can, become of humanity.

I.: If you could visit a past period, which one would you choose: two to ten years before your birth, 1900, 1700 to 1900, antiquity, or any other?

H.G.: Time of the cavemen—to see what most primitive creatures were like—the dawn of human consciousness. I choose it for the same reason as wanting to come back in 1,000 years. These are the periods we know least about.

I.: If you created a masterpiece, would you prefer 1,000 readers now or in 100 years?

H.G.: I'm not sure. I want to influence others through my work. Newton will be a relic in another 200 years. If they still read me in 100 years it probably means that my work was important in my own times.

I.: Are you afraid of death?

H.G.: A little—not much. I don't fear death. Nothingness does not bother me. But the reason why I feel anxious about it is that I am so involved in living, I want to go on living. I really don't fear death, but I want to live. However, I say that now, sitting here. In case of imminent danger, at the moment of being run over by a truck, I am sure I would have a fear response.

I.: How often do you think about your own death: daily, once a week, once a month, hardly ever?

H.G.: Probably once a week.

On the semantic differential rating scale, Gruber rated the meaning of death negatively, and the meaning of life highly positively.

Second Interview with Howard Gruber

After reading the transcribed interview, Professor Gruber felt that individual case studies should be treated in more depth. Thus, a few years after the original interview, I visited Dr. Gruber again to explore further his views on death. This session was taped. Though the discussion strayed at times from the main theme, I am rendering it in its entirety for two reasons:

1. It touches on many related thoughts and feelings about death that scientists all too seldom discuss seriously.
2. Since Gruber's main concern is the individual in his naked singularity, how can one do anything less than pursue his thoughts wherever they take us when it is Gruber himself whom we want to study?

After first re-reading the previous interview, Professor Gruber remarked that he still had to stick to the responses he had originally given, although he had a few reservations. He is "a little more nervous about time now," because he is somewhat older and also because he feels he is on the verge of a real breakthrough in the study of creativity.

I.: Is it important to you to finish what you are doing?

H.G.: I want to make progress. Finish? I don't think of finishing it. It's a long agenda! Related to the work on creativity is a specific work on evolving systems of thought. It also links up to a social philosophy that values the individual. And beyond that there are educational concerns that are also connected to my general approach to people.

I.: So you won't ever run out of projects?

H.G.: I can't imagine running out . . . I can't imagine finishing the job I have now set for myself.

I.: Can you conceive of ever exhausting your potential? Or do you think that we are open systems that can go on regenerating themselves forever?

H.G.: I just wrote a paper that has something to do with your idea of death. It's called "And the Bush Was not Consumed." I don't speak of death but about the "unquenchable flame." It says something about your last question.[4] One can't talk about human potential in general. In my particular

---

[4]A couple of weeks after the interview I received Dr. Gruber's (1979) paper. A paragraph on the very first page reads: "A creative moment is part of a longer creative process, which in its turn is part of a creative life. How are such lives lived? How can I express this peculiar idea that such an individual must be a self-regenerating system? Not a system that comes to rest when it has done good work, but one that urges itself onward. And yet, not a runaway system that accelerates its activity to the point where it burns itself out in one great flash. The system regulates the activity and the creative acts regenerate the system. The creative life happens in a being who can continue to work."

case, if by some mere miracle I finished all the projects now on my agenda, and it's a long list, I would replenish the agenda. But besides the intellectual functions, one needs optimism and a certain energy level. I can imagine becoming depleted but not the way I am functioning now, given my present energy level. If you would wave the magic wand and my agenda is complete, well, that would mean very little. I would have another agenda. So, for me to run out of projects would mean that I would have to become a different person on this dimension of optimism and energy. Now, I am granting that physical vigor and health—

I.: Let's forget about that for a moment. That always reminds me of the cliché, "The mind is willing, but the flesh is weak." Let us imagine that there is a consistency between the mental and physical potentials.

H.G.: Well, if my flesh doesn't weaken, my mind won't.

I.: It could go on forever?

H.G.: Well, when you say forever . . .

I.: All right, 300 years.

H.G.: My first answer is yes; the deepest part of me wants to say yes. But I have to leave a little room for some doubts. The doubts have to do with some personal and political disappointments I have suffered in life. For instance, a good, strong relation with a woman is an important thing for me. I am not sure how well I would do or, let us say, how well the system would go on if my hope gave out. Hope—I am not insisting that the actuality be there at every moment. I can imagine reaching a point where somehow or other I didn't have that or didn't have some substitute for it: my children or students around me, or a communal existence.[5]

I.: You are saying that under certain conditions you may not want to go on living. You may not be *interested* to be around regardless of your resources. What I have in mind is more of a teleological principle with all potentials there from the beginning. We just don't exhaust them because we always die before that happens, not because they are limitless, capable of renewing themselves forever. Can you conceive of ever reaching a point where you could say: "That's it; I have completed my life.

H.G.: I don't feel that way about it at all. It's not that I struggle so hard against death; I accept the fact that I am going to die, but to say that I am finished, that I am satisfied, that I would rather die than live—no! I would

---

[5]Gruber comes close to the concept of aphanisis as developed by Kurt Eissler (1955). It is the total extinction of all potentialities of pleasure. Eissler writes: "When this prospect [some future pleasure]—illusionary or realistic—crumbles, . . . death becomes the only solution, regardless of what the biological life potential of the person may still be."

distinguish two concepts in what you are saying. You said "limitless." I don't say limitless because that means infinite. I would say "indefinite." Human beings are finite; there is a limit to what I can do. If I finish certain things, the very fact of finishing them opens new horizons; I could build upon what I have finished, or I could open certain doors that I leave closed now.

I.: Thus, a life can never be experienced as complete?

H.G.: That seems very foreign to me. I think of structures of ideas as infinitely dense; inside of every idea is every other idea. There is an endless number of cross-sections through a structure of ideas. When you are talking of an individual or a collectivity of some kind, there will always be some new look you can take. Your teleological way of looking at things is alien to me. I recognize that there are things in me now that were recognizable in me when I was twelve years old, but there are other things that aren't. There are important ways in which I've changed. I think it was Joe North, a Communist political writer, who wrote: "A man should die pointed in his chosen direction struggling to get there." That's about the way I feel. And there is the Swedish film about the labor organizer, Joe Hill, who was executed by a firing squad. When he was blindfolded and tied to the pole, he struggled to get the blindfolds off—for a last look!

I.: Of course! His life was not completed. On the other hand, there is the story about Moreno, who, right after finishing his last book, said that he had done all he wanted to do. He simply went to bed, refused to eat, and died a few weeks later.

H.G.: Well, he was older.

I.: Yes, I think he was in his eighties.

H.G.: Well, you see, the reality is that when you are eighty, you do lose resources, energy, and so on; it just may no longer seem possible for you to do anything, to do something *new*. That might change the way you feel about the world. But you told me to leave the physical aspects out.

I.: If science were able to banish death one day, how would you feel about it? Would you banish death if you could?

H.G.: No. I have thought about that at times. When you talk with young people you frequently sense that they have not worked out a conception of life as a system. They have all sorts of completely unrealistic, fantastic ideas. Reaching the level of formal operations means being able to think seriously of what Piaget calls "the space of all possible things." It really means what's possible within some structured world, not just senseless fantasy. You have to put some limits on reality to make intelligent plans. You were asking me before about the chances of becoming depleted: but if you ask me how I am planning my life, that's an entirely different question. I am planning it around the idea that I am going to die. I know I am going to die and I want certain things to be accomplished, so I'm working within certain probabilities about getting old, losing my resources, my energy, to the point where I will have to retire and all that. I keep that in mind being thoroughly realistic, not thoroughly unrealistic. Now, let us look at the matter more generally: if there were no death, there could be no birth. At some point we must reach a limit to the size of the population; we would have a world of people getting older and older; there would be no babies; the whole process, the whole life cycle of birth and growing up and falling in love and making babies, and rearing the young—everything would change. What kind of world would that be? I haven't actually asked myself that question. Could you have a good world that would be like that? Would it in some sense be preferable to the one we have now? As a rough guess I would say it does not sound very appealing. So, if the price we pay for birth and growth and love is death, then we have to pay that price.

I.: Do you think of death as something out there, external to you, or is it internal, something within you?

H.G.: I really don't understand the question.

I.: Let's take Kastenbaum's [1972] example: you are sitting in your favorite chair, in your cozy study, reading, feeling very comfortable. Suddenly you feel an awesome presence behind you, as if death were there—it's like an alien force having invaded your familiar surroundings.

H.G.: Well, I never thought of it that personally; it's more remote for me than that. My life has been threatened. I was in World War II. But it hasn't been that close to me in that sense. That kind of death is external. I would say that when you talked about these two different sorts of imagery I could experience either kind. When you said "something inside you" I could immediately feel it clutching at me; that's one kind of imagery; or some kind of alien force inside of you rather than outside; that's really a third category. And I can also conceive of the winding-down idea of the way you describe Moreno. That's internal. But when you talked about death standing behind me, I can experience that too, as sort of an image; all of them are possible ways of thinking and feeling about it, if I have to think and feel about it. But I don't actually; it's more an abstract thing to me.

I.: It is not an experience?

H.G.: Well it will be now.

I.: Because we talked about it?

H. G.: Yes. If I look at the world in a new way I get a visual image of it. Once, when I was doing an experiment, I became acutely aware that the world tilts up. That is, visually, the ground on the horizon is at eye level. It goes from being at foot level at your feet to being at eye level at the horizon. From the moment it happened to me in a particular laboratory condition, I can now see it all the time. I can turn it on or off. I have a strong visual life. I look at the world with pleasure and very intensely, and I struggle to have a more inner visual life as well. Anyway, I have had a number of experiences like that, where I have some control of what I see; and I will be able to do that now with death. Maybe I will.

I.: You said that you actually don't think or "feel" about death—that it's more abstract to you . . .

H. G.: Well, I haven't been thinking about death a lot. I have been enjoying life and working hard and having fun . . . I should qualify that. The thought that has crossed my mind is, "well, if I have to die, at least my kids are grown up and at least I did get the Darwin book out." I did make one kind of unique statement personally and another kind professionally. If you were to tell me that I will die tomorrow, before I finish anything else, I would be a little less disappointed because of that. On the other hand, it all opens up again. I remember that when the Darwin book was nearly finished I used to think, "I'd better not get hit by a truck now; I've got to finish the book." All right, I finished the book; I didn't get hit by a truck, but I am beginning to have the same thought again. I have this creativity study well under way; besides, I am going to be a grandfather pretty soon. I want to be around. So you can talk about a phase of life finishing; and if somebody asks you, "well, how do you feel about dying?" you don't respond to your life as a whole, in a homogeneous way, but according to the phase you are at. When you are just finishing something, it's one thing and when you are just starting something, it's something else. It's a little bit like the Zeigarnik effect. It depends on where you are in moving through a set of tasks or an organization of purposes.

I.: That's very interesting. The way you put it, it's really cyclic. It all depends on where you are at the moment in life in relation to what you are doing. It depends on having just finished or having just begun. I think of it as much more accumulative: the more you have done, the easier it is to die.

H.G.: I wouldn't call it cyclic. I would say it is relative to where one stands in relation to a network of enterprises or a set of purposes.

I.: One finishes one and starts the next?

H.G.: Not really, because one doesn't do one thing at a time. Many of the questions that you ask about death relate to a person's purposes in life. Now I understand that there may be some people that don't have such a well-worked-out network of purposes. So the questions might look different to them. I have a variety of things that I am actually doing and some others that are bracketed and postponed. Every creative person, probably every human being, has a rather complex organization of purpose that he or she is moving through which is evolving as s/he goes along.

I.: Is "purpose" synonymous with "projects"?

H.G.: Projects are a bit too definite. Some of my energies have to be devoted to this "world betterment" side of things. Call it politics. I have mentioned political disappointments before. Having been a lifelong socialist, to see three socialist countries at war with each other in complicated ways— you can't help but be disappointed and confused as to what to do. You want to make a better world, but how? I don't claim to have an answer, but that doesn't mean that I'll stop looking. So a part of me that's saying "I am going to stay alive" means that I am going to go on looking. That's not exactly a project.

I.: Would you ever have been willing to die for a cause?

H.G.: Yes, I think so.

I.: Do you think that's a positive human quality?

H.G.: Yes. But I am a little cautious about it, because being ready to die is so close to being ready to kill that it makes me nervous.

I.: Don't you think that there would be no more wars if we were no longer willing to die for our causes? Aren't fanatics usually the ones who are most willing to die for their causes?

H.G.: No, I don't agree with that. The people who make wars are not the ones who fight them. The people who make wars—well sometimes *they* are fanatics. But wars come out of complex social systems. In any event, those who fight in wars don't die because they are fanatics. They die because they are afraid of the sergeants who stand behind them or they are afraid of what life would be like if they didn't follow orders. All right, there are some people who die for causes. I am not denying heroism, but that's not what makes wars.

I.: What about revolutions?

H.G.: Well, we are changing the grounds when we talk about the other kind of wars—small group struggles, revolutions. I don't really know how *real* death is to these people or how real it would be to me. To say that you are ready to die doesn't mean that you think you are going to die. Do you think that the probability is 99 out of 100 or one out of 100? Do we put it in these probabilistic terms at all? There are some cases where a person presses a grenade to his body and throws himself under a tank. He really knows that he is going to die.

I.: In the suicide squads they knew they were dying for their cause.

H.G.: Sometimes they just die for their squad. The shape of the motive is very complex. And that's one of the ways in which I have changed. If the way to achieve your political victory is through killing, I am very skeptical. That's what we are really talking about. We are not talking about death. We are talking about war and killing. And in the course of wars and killing, people die. If I participate, I might be one of those who kill, and I might be one of those who die. Giving my life for something is different from giving my death for it. You have really been asking me if I would give my death for something.

I.: What do you mean?

H.G.: Would I get into a situation where people are trying to kill each other? I might be the one who dies because I am trying to kill. I'm involved with other people who want to kill. In that sense I would be prepared to give my death in the struggle, but I am very dubious about that kind of struggle. If you ask me if I would give my life for it, that's another question.

I.: You would not hesitate to give your life for a better world?

H.G.: I would not hesitate. Now if you ask me if I know how to do that—what bank I am going to deposit my life in, so to speak—that's not so easy at this particular historical juncture. I am puzzled. So meanwhile, I fall back on something that has to be an ingredient of any worthwhile solution: treasuring individual human life. That's where my work in creativity is relevant. The point is, it's not that I feel my life is so important, and not someone else's. Every human life is, but mine too.

I.: Isn't mine more important than anyone else's? Is anything really more important than one's own life?

H.G.: Let's make it more concrete. What about the standard example: your child is just about to be run over and you push the child out of the way, endangering your own life.

I.: You don't know what you would do in such a moment. If you do it, it is not because you feel your life is less important. It's an instinctive reaction. But let us assume the child needs one of my organs to survive, and I know that the transplant will kill me. Could I make this ultimate commitment?

H.G.: Well, the question I ask myself immediately is how would I live if I didn't do it, if my child died? I have to create my life so that I can live with it. I thought about that when I read these stories about cannibalism among marooned people. They are very gripping. My problem is: how does one live afterwards? I don't know that I could.

I.: That's different! Not giving up my heart or liver is not the same as killing someone to survive. There again, one can't know beforehand how one would react. This may be a case of survival of the stronger or the fitter, not of sacrificing one's life for someone. I imagine that neither would be likely to kill the other.

H.G.: One creative solution would be for either one of them to say: "A" will not kill me. We will both die because I can't kill him, so I'll kill myself.

I.: Yes, but he is not sacrificing his life for anyone. It isn't altruism. It may be simply easier than to kill, easier than to engage in cannibalism to survive. It's still not the same as giving up a vital organ.

H.G.: I don't think there would be a good life left for me in either case if I didn't make that sacrifice. Here I can say "sacrifice." Giving up the organ would really be equivalent to killing myself on a desert island so that "A" can survive.

I.: I perceive the two cases as entirely different. But let us postulate a third situation: imagine that you lived in a dictatorship and the secret police came to your house to take a hostage: you or your son. To say "take my son" is in no way the same thing as to refuse to donate my liver or my heart or whatever.

H.G.: Why not?

I.: It's not just a question of surviving or not surviving.

H.G.: Now here we have three cases: the prospective cannibalism; the organ donation; and the hostage problem. All seem alike to me, even though there are important differences emotionally; but they are the same as far as what I have to do. I don't automatically say that I would die; it would depend on who the people are. But I am not comfortable saying that. It places differential values on different lives.

I.: I have asked people if their death would be easier to take if they knew that (1) the world would continue to go on as it has in the past; (2) the world will be a better place to live in; (3) the time of their death coincided with the end of all life on earth.

H.G.: That doesn't seem relevant because death doesn't seem so hard to me.

I.: You have also said that you would die for a better world.

H.G.: But that is not the same question. At any moment of my life, including the last one, I would be happier to think the world would be better and very unhappy to think the world would come to an end. But that has nothing to do with my death . . . I don't see death as hard. You are asking a specific question: is death easier or harder under specific conditions? Well, I don't want to die, but death does not seem "a hard thing." If we turned the question around: if I were the last person alive after the whole world had been destroyed by some nuclear war, and life had no prospect of any pleasure, no human intercourse, I don't think I would mind dying.

I.: But you are greatly concerned about a better world, even if you know you will no longer be around. You can't say, *"après moi, le déluge."*

H.G.: Oh no, no, not at all!

I.: Do you think that having children makes any difference?

H.G.: Well, if you had asked me if there is anything that makes dying easier, I would have said, "having children." I am surprising myself saying it because I had just denied that death was difficult. The experience of having been a father, having raised my children, having been involved with their lives—I guess that is the most fulfilling thing in my whole life. I can say *"après moi, quelque chose,"* rather than *"le déluge."* After all, my children go on. I don't want the end of the world under any circumstances but also because they will be there.

I.: Is there an immortality factor involved?

H.G.: I don't know if it's the same thing as immortality. I am aware that it might be implied in what I was just saying. I don't know if that's how I think about it. My children are so different from each other and from me. Is it really me that will live on in them? That seems excessively narcissistic.

I.: Do you feel that they are part of you?

H.G.: I rather feel that I am part of them. I feel invested in their lives. Not so much that a part of me is surviving, but that those new creatures are there and I want them to go on. I haven't clearly worked that out. I don't feel that I live on in a child, but in an abstract way I can say I have conveyed certain values. They wouldn't be who they are if they hadn't lived with me for twenty years.

I.: How about your book on Darwin? Would it mean anything to you to know that people will still read it in a 100 years?

H.G.: I don't know if it does. It depends; if they read it 100 years from now as a curiosity, it means that it was a failure. If they read it because it helped to change things, and things moved in a certain direction because of my work, well, that's entirely different. But then it doesn't matter if they read it or not. The more I am a success, the less it matters that my particular work be read.

I.: What about the assurance that people will still know your name—does that mean anything?

H.G.: I really will be dead. I really won't know.

Karl H. Pribram, Psychologist, Psychiatrist, Physiologist

Biography

Karl H. Pribram received his M.D. degree at the University of Chicago in 1941 at the age of twenty-two and became certified in the specialty of neurological surgery. However, most of his career over the past three decades had been devoted to brain/behavior research, which he pursued at the Yerkes Laboratories of Primate Biology while Karl Lashley was director; at Yale University, where Pribram taught neurophysiology and physiological psychology; and for the past twenty years at Stanford University, where he is professor of neuroscience in the departments of psychology and of psychiatry and behavioral sciences.

He has held appointments as honorary lecturer and visiting scholar at the most prestigious institutes and universities throughout the United States and Canada, as well as at the universities of Leningrad, Moscow, and London. Many of the books he has authored, co-authored, or edited have become classics in the fields of psychology, physiology, and brain research. He has also published a number of essays that attempt to deal with the mind–brain problems from a scientific vantage.

However, Professor Pribram has become best known in the international scientific community for his revolutionary model of the human brain, based on the concept of the hologram, which has been hailed as a major breakthrough in theories of memory and perception.

The extraordinary span of professional activity is reflected by his memberships and fellowships in professional societies such as American Physiological Association, American Medical Association, American Academy of Psychoanalysis, and Society for Experimental Psychologists; Pribram is a member of the Central Council of the Internation Brain Research Organization, a former president of the International Neuropsychological Society, and a past president of the Division of Physiological and Comparative Psychology of the American Psychological Association, to name just a few. Pribram's enormously broad areas of research are also reflected in his current editorships: *Neuropsychologia; Journal of Mathematical Biology; Advances in Behavioral Biology; Human Motivation; International Journal of Neuroscience; Journal of Neuroscience Research; The Behavioral and Brain Sciences; Journal of Mental Imagery*.

Interview

I.: What is your *ultimate* goal in life?

K.P.: To make an impact on the development of our culture.

I.: How important is it to reach this goal? How much would you be willing to sacrifice for its sake?

K.P.: One must keep a balance between how much one can sacrifice and still remain creative. I would make sacrifices to the extent that they do not damage creativity.

I.: What is your most important time orientation: past, present, or future?

K.P.: The future.

I.: How long do you *expect* to live?

K.P.: To about ninety-five.

I.: How long would you *prefer* to live?

K.P.: A little longer than that.

I.: If after you died you could come back once, when would you choose to come back: 2, 10, 100, or 1,000 years after your death?

K.P.: In what condition? For how long a time?

I.: In your present condition, and for a relatively short time. Just for a visit; to look around for a while.

K.P.: Would I have my memory—I mean of my present life?

I.: Funny, no one ever asked this question. Yes, let's assume with your memory.

K.P.: In 1,000 years.

I.: For what reason did you choose 1,000 years?

K.P.: I could find out what had intervened between then and now—and so the further in the future the better.

I.: If you could visit a period in the past, which one would you choose: two to ten years before your birth; 1900, 1700 to 1900; antiquity, or any other period?

K.P.: Way back, to the origin of mankind. I would love to see how we began.

I.: Are you afraid of death?

K.P.: I have to answer this in two ways, yes and no. I organize my life in a way so that things are in good shape. At the moment everything is in order. In this respect I do not fear death. But, on the other hand, there are still so many things that are not *yet* done; so many things I still want to do. I am not finished.

I.: Can you conceive of ever feeling that you have finished all you wanted to do? Do you think that if we lived long enough, we would eventually exhaust all our potentials?

K.P.: Not really. At times one hits plateaus, but they are only plateaus. Eventually one regenerates again.

I.: And this regeneration can go on forever?

K.P.: Yes, I think so.

I.: Would you favor banishing death, if we were able to do so?

K.P.: Yes. I would want to stay alive indefinitely.

I.: How about everybody? If we could all become immortal?

K.P.: Yes. If we could bring that about, I would want to contribute towards our survival. Of course, that's part of a physician's commitment anyway.

I.: What about the consequences our immortality would have on the quality of life: Overpopulation, starvation, stagnation. No death could mean no more birth; no renewal . . .

K.P.: I don't think that these are necessary consequences. I rather envision that we could meet every new challenge. Our resources and our potentials are limitless, we just haven't tapped them. Whenever a problem presents itself, we can find ways to solve it. Perhaps we can expand, establish space stations. We must go ahead, change, progress . . .

I.: Would life not lose its value, if there were no longer death? If there were always a tomorrow, would we do anything today?

K.P.: Ah, that's a different question. We may very well need death as the motivating principle of life. Death does lend value to life.

I.: How often do you think about your own death: daily, once a week, once a month, or hardly ever?

K.P.: Every few years it comes to mind.

I.: Are you serious? You hardly ever think about your own death?

K.P.: I don't think about death for years. If you call that "hardly ever," then that's what it is.

I.: If you could have chosen a period in which to live your life, which one would you have chosen: your own period, a past one, or a future one?

K.P.: My own period.

On the semantic differential rating scale, Pribram rated the meaning of death negatively and the meaning of life highly positively.

7

Further Analysis of the Interviews

Common Threads

In our interviews and comments so far, we have focused on the uniqueness of each individual and on the individual's idiosyncratic way of dealing with his own finiteness. However, while Milstein does not resemble Stern, nor does Wheeler resemble Wigner, the high level of self-actualization and the exceptional creativity they share manifests itself in common threads that are woven through their interviews, binding them together and setting them apart from most other groups of people we interviewed. Thus, after having recognized the variations in individual views and experiences, we now turn our attention to common threads.

Reading through the set of interviews, it becomes evident that scientists are overwhelmingly future-oriented and have greatly expanded time perspectives. We need only recall their general preference for a visit 1,000 years hence and their interest in going as far back as the earliest eras of human existence, or even further. But one could argue that the scientists' time orientation is a peculiarity of their profession rather than a reflection of their attitudes toward death. One major purpose of scientific endeavor is, after all, to predict future occurrences. And one of the tools of prediction is the understanding of past events. Thus, a predominantly future orientation together with an extended time perspective could be explained along these lines. Of course, we would still be faced with the question of whether one is more likely to become a scientist because one has a vast time perspective or whether one acquires the time perspective as a consequence of being a scientist. But how do we explain the scientists' expressed lack of interest in their own past, closely resembling the artists in this respect?

Interestingly, a connection can be drawn between the artists' prevalent choice not to return at all after death nor to visit any pre-birth period, and the scientists' interest in returning after a thousand years and of visiting antiquity or the dawn of mankind: these responses all demonstrate a readiness to surrender life. These choices are particularly significant when we remember that the most frequently chosen interval by all other groups of people interviewed was two to ten years after death.

The differences between the artists' and the scientists' choices reflect in part the greater self-involvement or self-directedness of the artist, who seems uninterested in a time "when he is not." This is expressed in a nutshell by Stern's remark, "après moi, le déluge." In addition, one of the scientists' major characteristics is "other-directedness," "world-directedness," or, more simply, curiosity.

Through responses to the question "How often do you think about your own death?" it became evident that the scientists were more preoccupied with death on a conscious level than were the artists. Half of the artists maintained that they "hardly ever" thought of death, while only one scientist said that he rarely thought about it.

Does the scientist's readiness to think and talk about his death imply that he is more at ease with his mortality than the artist? I do not think so.

Internal Versus External Locus of Death

The difference just noted in conscious preoccupation with death might very well be related to the fact that two different modes of experiencing the locus of death exist: the internal and the external. We can experience death as a friendly or a hostile force lurking somewhere in the world, a force which will eventually embrace or attack us. Or we can experience it within ourselves as an integral part of our being, something that has coexisted with our lives from the very beginning.[1]

[1]One may argue that death can not be experienced one way or another since "experience" and "death" are mutually exclusive: experience is a conscious act and death is nothingness or unself-consciousness. But one of the most remarkable facets of the human mind is the ability to experience events *in absentia*. We experience our fantasies, dreams, and hallucinations. My intuitions and anticipations can be just as vivid and real (or fabricated) as my memories. Our experiences are limited only by our imagination.

Kastenbaum and Aisenberg (1972) have described the following death experience. "I am sitting in my study, thinking, reading, feeling comfortable and at ease in my familiar surrounding. Suddenly, I feel the presence of an alien force—it has no name—it is nothing—yet in some way I feel it behind me, touching me. Death is there. The alien force has intruded into my intimate surrounding." Here, of course, the locus of death is external, an experience with which we are much more familiar. Not only have wars and diseases been portrayed as killers approaching us from a hostile environment, but since early childhood we have been exposed to more or less sophisticated death symbols and death personifications: skulls, skeletons, scythes, sorcerers, vampires, dying swans, tolling bells, dances of death, dirges, hourglasses, and clocks. All these, and many more, represent death waiting in the wings.

In every age the artist creates new images and recreates many of the old ones. But to be able to externalize death, it must have been internalized first. Goethe remarked that "what is outside must be inside." Perhaps one of the necessary conditions for a true artist is a multitude of images and experiences emanating from within rather than from without. But death as an internal force is much harder to describe. It can't be set into a scene like the one illustrated by Kastenbaum and Aisenberg, since death within is not punctuated by appearances and disappearances. *It is always there.*

Robert Lifton (1976) has described the *hibakusha* (Hiroshima survivors) as having a keen awareness of carrying death within them. But one need not be contaminated or diseased to locate death within oneself. In existential analysis, especially Heidegger's, our entire existence rests on the presence of death in each moment of life. Part of the totality of our lives is the not-yet-existing, which includes death. "Running ahead to my own death" (Heidegger's "being-toward-death"), of which we may or may not be aware, leads to our authenticity.

In a discussion in support of the Freudian death instinct, Eissler's (1955) quotes of Simmel (1918) and Rilke (1950) are good examples of death viewed as an internal force. Simmel had observed that the locus of death in Shakespearean characters depended on their importance. Subordinate figures die as a consequence of some external event; they are somehow killed. But the great tragic heroes "are allowed to die from within; the maturation of their destinies as an expression of life is per se the maturation of their deaths." The second quotation Eissler cites, the most succinct description that I have encountered of death within, is a line in a poem by Rilke (written in 1925), in which he announces his approaching death to a friend. He writes, "The ego founders upon the id," a confirmation of Freudian thanatology.[2]

Clearly, our conceptions and experiences of death as without or within vary. Of course, death can also be viewed as existing no-where—can "nothing" be anywhere? Or we can experience it every-where if we feel it surrounding us from without and trapping us within. Our concern here is not with locating death correctly but with understanding the consequences of these different modes of experi-ence. Of interest here is Gruber's response to locating death: "I have not thought of death in such a personal way. But now that I have imagined it, I'll be able to experience it both ways."

All of the above leads us to conclude that death can be repre-sented both within and without. But, individually, we tend to cultivate one image while negating the other. And death viewed as an external event—as an accident—is a defense against what is a more threatening image of death for most of us: death as an inner necessity, from which there is no escape. But as Marcuse has stated so well, "Man is not free as long as death has not become really 'his own'; that is, as long as it has not been brought under his autonomy." Death, thus conceived, becomes an end in itself—the goal of life—rather than a "redemption from life."

If artists are indeed more likely to locate death within themselves while scientists tend to view death as an external force, the observed differences in needs and orientation of these two groups of people would be understandable. Thus, if death is an intimate part of my life, my steady companion, of which I have been aware as much or as little as I am aware of the air I breathe, I should be less preoccupied with it than if it is conceived as an external force which is coming irrevocably closer. My need to fathom it, talk about it, fight it, shun it, or join

---

[2]Although nothing can be more "internal" than an instinct, Freud's thanatology has some confusing elements in it. The oft-quoted statement that there is no representation of our own death in the unconscious was written in 1915 (*Thoughts for the Times on War and Death*). But in *Beyond the Pleasure Principle* (1920), which contains the final revision of his theory of instincts, we read that "everything living dies for internal reasons" and that "the aim of all life is death."

it—like an enemy or a friend—will probably be greater in the latter case. If, furthermore, I am capable of giving form to that facet of my life—my death—by converting the abstract experience into a concrete production, I will externalize or project my innermost feelings through artistic creation. Meanwhile, the need to express my relationship with death by other means should be lessened.

Interestingly, preoccupation with death is not related to fear of death. Individuals who claim to fear death maintain just as frequently that they hardly ever think about their death as that they think about it daily. The same holds true for those who claim not to be afraid of death.

Intrinsic Versus Extrinsic Motivation

With very few exceptions, both scientists and artists seem relatively at ease with their lives, including the prospect of death. Not only did their responses indicate a much higher level of having come to terms with death than those given by the majority of individuals in every other group; on a nonverbal level as well there emerges an unmistakable quality of ego-syntony, a feeling that one is in harmony with oneself and with one's environment. This sharply contradicts the stereotyped image of the complex, high-strung, tense, highly creative individual.[3] Nor was there any resignation. Instead, the most commonly shared characteristic of the creative individuals was their enthusiasm and the pleasure they took in whatever they were doing. Their activity is invariably an end in itself, rather than a means to an end. This is expressed most dramatically by Wigner:" . . . I don't feel that my work is 'important.' I mean *vitally* important. I love the work. I am interested in it for its own sake, not because I believe it is important."

This is an expression of purely intrinsic motivation; it was shared by all the artists and scientists. Also, none could set limits as to how far they would go or how much they would sacrifice for the sake of artistic or scientific endeavors, since it was inconceivable to let anything

[3]One may object that only those relatively at ease with themselves agreed to be interviewed. In this respect our sample is biased. But the same bias holds true for all other people who were interviewed. Everyone was told about the topic beforehand and had to agree to be interviewed. Some refused in almost every group.

interfere with them. As a matter of fact, the term "sacrifice" was rejected repeatedly. Goals, almost without exception, related to work and accomplishments and were often equated with "life itself."

This is in sharp contrast to the extrinsically motivated majority of respondents, including successful people who report "liking" or "loving" their vocation. In most cases, they express a willingness to make a *limited* amount of *sacrifices*—most often in terms of work, study, economizing—to achieve limited goals. Work, for the most part, is a means to an end, rather than an end in itself. Some typical responses are: "I would be willing to work my head off for the next X years to achieve true financial security." "I would be ready to do almost anything for a 'Beverly Hills' life-style." "A good family life is the most important thing. But there is nothing I can do about it. It's fate." With few exceptions, in all but the highly creative individuals, investments to achieve one's goals ranged from statements such as "I don't want to make any *sacrifices*" or "I really can't make *sacrifices*" to "I would make any necessary *sacrifice*."

The most frequently mentioned goals by all people interviewed to date except the artists and scientists were financial security, material possessions, and a good "family life" followed by accomplishment (increasing understanding, education, etc.) and fame. Power was rarely mentioned as an ultimate goal. Interestingly, material goals were just as often chosen by the wealthy as by the poor—but never by any of the highly creative people—while the "good family life" was mentioned with equal frequency by all interviewees including the artists and scientists.

But how do these different motivational orientations develop in the first place? We shall avoid the heredity–environment controversy by taking for granted that motivation is present in all humans long before a specific form of it has taken shape. Possibly one must have experienced an activity before that activity can become an end in itself, rather than a means to an end.[4]

Several of the musicians I interviewed stated that they could not

---

[4]But even this assumption is open to doubt. Thus, thumb-sucking may very well be done for its own sake, for the pure enjoyment of the activity from the very beginning, rather than for the release of tension.

remember a time when they had no goal, a goal frequently set for them by their parents. But would they have internalized these goals without their extraordinary talents? Probably not. The feeling of accomplishing something uniquely their own, doing it better than anyone else, leaving a mark, is certainly an important factor in the development that leads to equating one's work with life itself.

However, there are many highly gifted people who do not invest all their resources in the development of talent or in the pursuit of self-actualizing goals. The most critical difference between extrinsically and intrinsically motivated individuals can be expressed in terms of the freedom to pursue their goals. In the former there are obvious restraints: striving, needs, and goals are more or less successfully balanced and limited by the investment one dares to make and one is able to make; in the latter, the sky is the limit. The urge "to do one's thing" is an inner necessity which knows no restraint; all one's potentials are thrown toward self-actualization. Graham conveys this sentiment when he says, "There are no limits. Whatever you really want, you must want it irrationally. . . . You can't set any limits on the effort you are willing to put into it."

It may sound paradoxical, but freedom to act as one desires is possible only with control—control over one's resources, the ability to channel one's energy in the direction one chooses. This is a rare quality! The realization of the degree to which most people *cannot* do what they really want to do became shockingly clear in the responses the nonartists and nonscientists gave concerning their goals. The obstacles expressed are primarily in terms of inhibitions, self-consciousness, lack of strength, fears, and anxieties. Frequently occurring statements were: "It's there [the talent or knowledge] but I just can't express it," "I get all tense," or "I get all choked up." "I can't get myself to really follow through with it," "It's too late now," "I don't have the energy it takes," or "I am too exhausted." "It's too much of a risk." "There is something holding me back." "It's all fate anyway—it's not under my control."

What seems to be lacking in so many cases is the daring to live and to give generously of oneself—and also the courage to take whatever life has to offer. If one tiptoes timidly through life, putting one's eggs into many baskets and taking them out again before they are hatched, one is being prudent; but then life will hardly lead to the ecstatic experience of fulfillment.

The following six interviews constitute a cross-section of people at various stages of self-fulfillment and fear of death. They demonstrate the startling qualitative differences between truly creative lives and all others.

8

Selected Interviews: The Unfulfilled

Three Aimless Lives

Christian Bart[1]

Christian Bart is a Swiss banker who lives in Zurich and in Palm Beach, Florida. About thirty years ago he lost one leg in an automobile race. The accident brought about a drastic change in his self-concept and in his life-style. For many, many years Mr. Bart has been an ardent theosophist. At the time of the interview he was sixty-two years old.

> **I.:** What do you conceive as the height of fulfillment, as your ultimate goal?
>
> **C.B.:** To take one step forward toward ultimate reality.
>
> **I.:** How much would you sacrifice to attain this goal?
>
> **C.B.:** Everything, gladly.
>
> **I.:** Do you live primarily in the past, the present, or the future?
>
> **C.B.:** I am eagerly awaiting the future. I am not very interested in the here and now. That is, I am interested insofar as it prepares me for the future. I am somewhat more involved with the past.
>
> **I.:** How long do you expect to live?
>
> **C.B.:** A very short time; at most four more years.

---

[1] To assure anonymity the names of people, places, and affiliations have been changed slightly, while otherwise perserving all important characteristics.

I.: Do you have any reason for such a short life expectancy?

C.B.: No, not at all. I am in very good health. It's just an intuition. Perhaps it's what I really desire.

I.: You mean you would prefer to die soon?

C.B.: Yes, I am ready to die any time. I would resent getting old.

I.: If after you died you could come back once for a short period of time, would you choose to come back 2, 10, 100, or 1,000 years after your death?

C.B.: Two years, so that I can look after my family.

I.: I mean just for a short time. Just to look around.

C.B.: Yes, I would still choose two years. The longer intervals I will see anyway. But reincarnation takes a long time. That time, the time "out of body" is used to process all the material, which is very good. But on the other hand, if one can come back soon, there is still a continuation, one is still in touch.

I.: If you could visit a past period, which one would you choose: two to ten years before your birth, 1900, 1700 to 1900, antiquity, or any other?

C.B.: The eighteenth century. That's when I was last here.

I.: Are you afraid of death?

C.B.: No. I would be afraid of immortality in my present personality. And I don't think my life is of such great value. It's just a vehicle to gather experiences.

I.: How often do you think about your own death?

C.B.: It's very much on my mind. Not every day but at least once a week.

I.: If you could have chosen the time in which to live, would you have preferred a period in the past, the future, or your own time?

C.B.: I would have chosen a period in the future.

On the semantic differential rating scale, Mr. Bart glorified death by attributing only highly positive qualities to it, while he evaluated life as somewhat less positive than death.

Steven Burek

Steven Burek is a thirty-six-year-old electrical engineer. He has been with IBM since he graduated from City College in New York. He lives alone, in a studio in Greenwich Village.

S.B.: My goal in life? Oh, I don't know—I really want many things.

I.: What about professionally related goals?

S.B.: Well, they could be. But I would rather "make it" in something more exciting.

I.: How much would you be willing to sacrifice to attain these goals?

S.B.: That's hard to say. I am always wasting a lot of time. I could certainly forgo a lot of things, I mean abstain from daily little pleasures, be more disciplined, to achieve my goals. But I don't do much planning. I don't think of the future. I really live from day to day.

I.: What is your most important time dimension? Past, present, or future?

S.B.: Definitely the present. The future makes me nervous. I am not dissatisfied with what I have achieved, but I don't see myself going anywhere. And my past certainly was not so great either. I don't think much about it.

I.: How long do you expect to live?

S.B.: I have no expectations, no intuition whatever, other than that the end is still very far off.

I.: What is your preference regarding time of death?

S.B.: Oh, far in the future.

I.: If after you died you could come back once for a short period, when would you choose to come back: 2, 10, 100, or 1,000 years after your death?

S.B.: Ten years. No, not really; two years would be better. Things are always changing too much. If I waited any longer there would be too many changes.

I.: If you could visit a past period, which one would you choose: two to ten years before your birth, 1900, 1700 to 1900, antiquity, or any other?

S.B.: Around 1900, because things were not so different then. Life was already more convenient, civilized, and comfortable.

I.: Are you afraid of death?

S.B.: No. I don't concern myself with it. It's too far in the future.

I.: How often do you think about your own death?

S.B.: I really don't think about it.

I.: Do you think you would sacrifice your life for anything; for a person, for a cause . . .

S.B.: I don't know for sure. I don't think so.

I.: If you knew you had only one year to live, would you make any changes in your life-style?

S.B.: Yes, I certainly would. For one thing, I would contact a lot of people, see everybody I once knew—like completing a cycle. I would also indulge myself. Do anything I wanted to do. I certainly would quit my job immediately, even if I had to make some debts. But I would have to be sure that I really have to die within the year.

He attributed slightly more positive qualities than negative ones to both life and death on the semantic differential rating scale.

Harry Pitt

Harry Pitt, a fifty-three-year-old alcoholic, has been unemployed for a little over a year. He had held many different jobs as a laborer. During the last five years he ran his own parking lot. He finally sold the lot, as he was not physically fit to continue working.

I.: What do you *really* want out of life? What is the most important goal?

H.P.: To make a good living.

I.: How much would you sacrifice to make it?

H.P.: I have no will power. I don't mind working hard and working long hours, but I know that I can't make any real sacrifices. And anyway, there isn't anything I do well.

I.: Do you live mostly in the present, the past, or the future?

H.P.: I live completely in the past.

I.: How come? Was it that good?

H.P.: No, not really. But the present is worse and I am afraid of what the future will bring.

I.: How long do you *expect* to live?

H.P.: Not very long. I'll die before I get very old.

I.: What is your preference regarding time of death?

H.P.: In old, old age. But before my wife dies. I couldn't live alone.

I.: If after you died you could come back once for a short period, when would you choose to come back: 2, 10, 100, or 1,000 years after your death?

H.P.: Two years. I would like to see how my wife and her grandchildren are doing. I sure wish I could come back.

I.: If you could visit a period in the past, would you choose two to ten years before your birth, 1900, 1700 to 1900, ancient times, or any other?

H.P.: The eighteen hundreds. That was a time when it was still possible to make something of yourself.

I.: Are you afraid of death?

H.P.: Yes, terribly afraid. I have been [afraid] for the last thirty years. Can't sleep at all, after a funeral. I hate to leave the family. I am also afraid of being buried, of the unknown, of judgment day; I am even afraid to go to sleep—I might not wake up. It's better when I drink. I don't worry so much. But then I worry afterwards, because the drinking will kill me even sooner. If I had another chance, I would do things differently. But I really never had a chance.

I.: How often do you think about your own death?

H.P.: Every day. Certainly every night.

I.: If you had a choice when to live, would you prefer a period in the past, in the future, or your own period?

H.P.: A period in the future, because there will be more opportunities.

On the semantic differential rating scale, Mr. Pitt evaluated death extremely negatively and life as highly positive.

Analysis

At first glance these three people seem to have nothing in common. Christian Bart is a well educated upper-class European, who seems to be welcoming death. Steven Burek, a middle-class American "company" man, claims not to be aware of death since it's too far off. And finally, Harry Pitt, a social drop-out has been terrified of death all his life. While one of them espouses the most lofty goals, matched by a readiness to make supreme sacrifices for their sake, another one feels powerless even to attempt striving toward the most parochial of goals. Furthermore, they appear to live in different "time zones," focusing respectively on the future, the present, and the past. However, despite these obvious differences, the three interviews resemble each other more than they do any of the twenty preceding ones. I do not think one can read them without becoming keenly aware that all three are highly unfulfilled individuals, having resigned themselves to the fact that this life does not hold much in store for them.

To begin with, Christian Bart's future orientation, so rarely encountered in any but creative people, turns out, on closer examination, to be "other-worldly," serving as an escape from the reality of the present. He has come to terms with death by devaluating life and by viewing death as redemption from it. His energies and talents are largely invested in maintaining his defensive structure. Only the fantasy question belies his disinterest in the here and now. He would choose to return to this life as soon as possible, to "look after" his family, and he is interested in the "continuation" of life on earth as he knows it.

Steven Burek's main emphasis on the present is also an escape—an escape from a past and a future, which he views as even less tolerable than the present. He is like one slightly sick on a roller coaster. It is all right as long as one does not look forward or backward; nowhere to turn, nothing to do but hang on! He does not like any changes, but neither does he like things as they are. (We have only to remember the drastic changes he would make in his life-style if he had only one year to live.) He wastes his energies on repressing his fears and dissatisfactions and is thus incapable of channeling them into productive, self-actualizing activity.

Harry Pitt is by far the least self-fulfilled individual of the three. Besides lacking objectively in internal as well as external resources, he also lacks the most rudimentary defensive structure. Alcohol is his only escape from terror. Dynamically, his mode of "living in the past" is not so different from Mr. Burek's emphasis on the present or Mr. Bart's focus on the future. They all are attempting to escape from the traumatic experiences of having wasted their lives.

We see here how three different responses—claiming a future, a present, and a past orientation, respectively—can have similar meanings. They dramatically demonstrate how misleading inferences can be when based on single responses taken out of context. Only in the responses to the fantasy question, where neither education nor defense mechanisms come into play, do the most basic similarities manifest themselves. Bart's choice to return two years after his death is surprising. It does not seem to fit in with the rest of the interview, which conveys a lack of interest in this life, perhaps even a desire to die. Yet he would like to return at a time when he is "still in touch" and when he can look after his family. Burek wants to come back soon enough to be sure everything is still the same; and Pitt wishes fervently for a speedy return, since he cannot tolerate the idea of being separated from his family.

All three express not only a dissatisfaction with life, but more importantly, a lack of any trust in their ability to achieve some measure of self-fulfillment. This lack of self-fulfillment is often externalized to represent a harsh world which rejects their attempts and hopes. "Fate," then, overcomes their dreams, and they respond to it with the hopelessness of those whose lives have been surrendered prematurely.

These interviews are certainly not typical of the several hundred conducted. I deliberately chose them for their striking contrast to the interviews with artists and scientists. But before drawing any further conclusions about differences between highly self-actualized individuals and those less so, we shall look at three more interviews. The first is with a twenty-three-year-old who committed suicide about six months after this interview took place. The two others are well-functioning individuals, whose responses closely match those which most frequently occur in interviews with people assessed as ranking in the medium-high range of the self-actualization dimension.

The Social Drop-out

Billy Bulka had spent many of his adolescent and young adult years in correctional institutions. He was one of the younger siblings in a family of ten children. He traced his problems back to seventh grade, the time he began to realize that he was taller, stronger, handsomer, and smarter than most, including his teachers; that his schoolmates tended to be afraid of him, while the girls vied for his attention and protection; that he could really do whatever he wanted to do; and finally that his mother's affection was unattainable, regardless of his behavior. According to Bulka, his troubles started with playing hooky and running errands for his "bookie" father and brothers. Before long, he was dealing with drugs and becoming himself addicted. He shoplifted, committed battery and knifings, and attempted robberies. At the time of the interview he was on a methadone program, in psychotherapy, and trying hard to change his life.

I.: What is the highest goal in your life?

B.B.: At this moment, financial security. But that wouldn't satisfy me in the long run. I would really love to establish some facility that would help others—mostly kids. I would want to create and direct something that is *big* and does good.

I.: How far would you be willing to go, or how much would you be willing to sacrifice toward that goal?

B.B.: I can't say. I am not very good at making sacrifices. I would certainly not sacrifice my wife or my family.

I.: Do you live mostly in the past, the present, or the future?

B.B.: I am not sure. A great deal in the past—thinking how things could have been different. I think back to the days in school. If only I had continued my education. A lot of regrets about the past. But there were also good times. I was a big shot at sixteen. All the money I wanted. Boy, did I blow it!

I.: What about the future? Making some plans for it?

B.B.: No. It's really useless. I don't have a chance. When I think about the future—I don't know—it's like looking into a black tunnel. But the present is important. It's sometimes even good. I got tickets to a baseball game. I *love* the Yankees.

I.: How long do you *expect* to live?

B.B.: That depends. *If* I make it to thirty, I will make it. I mean, I would have a normal life, and a natural death. I wouldn't get as old as my father will, because of all the things I have done to myself, but I would live a normal lifetime. But I don't think I will make it to thirty.

I.: How long would you want to live? What is your preference?

B.B.: Between sixty and seventy is enough. I don't want to get real old.

I.: If after you died you could come back once for a short period, when would you choose to come back: 2, 10, 100, or 1,000 years after your death?

B.B.: Two years. To see my family. But I would really like to choose a week, so that I can let them know what it is like. I have sometimes thought how great it would be to see my own funeral. See if people mourn my passing. I really would love to see it!

I.: If you could visit a past period—before you were born—which would you choose: two to ten years before your birth, 1900, 1700 to 1900, antiquity, or any other?

B.B.: 1929. To see the Yankees play the World Series.

I.: Are you afraid of death?

B.B.: No. It's going to come—there is nothing to stop it—nothing that we can do. And I believe in God. There must be something better than this. Anyway, there is no sense fearing it—may as well go there "swinging" it.

I.: How often do you think about your own death: daily, once a week, once a month, hardly ever?

B.B.: Perhaps three times a month or once a week.

I.: If you could have chosen a period in which to live, would you have preferred a period in the past, a period in the future, or your own time?

B.B.: A period in the past. That was much better.

On the semantic differential rating scale, Bulka rated death more positively than life.

This interview contains a number of warning signals of an impending desperate action. Previously, Bulka had told his therapist of a grand scheme he had to kidnap her, collect $20,000 in ransom, and make off for South America. Though he certainly had no intention of carrying it out, he wanted to be taken seriously. He went into the most minute details of his kidnaping plan, reassuring the therapist that no harm could befall *him* (not her), "It's real easy and completely foolproof. Nothing to it!" But as an afterthought he remarked, "I really shouldn't have told you about it if I really want to do it, but I don't! I really don't want to leave here. Everybody I know is here. And it wouldn't do any good, anyway. What would I do there? The same that I have been doing here. It's too late. There is nothing I can do to change my life."

During the months following the interview, Bulka made several unsuccessful suicide attempts and each time was released from the hospital after a day or two. He told his therapist: "It's hard to die. It takes a great deal of courage to take your own life. People always say it's cowardly—but I know now that it isn't. And it's also hard to succeed at it. I have taken ten times as many drugs as anyone else would need to kill himself, and nothing happens. I must be immune to everything, and I don't have the guts to jump out of a window." A few weeks before his successful suicide attempt, he was persuaded to commit himself to a county hospital. But a week later he was discharged for having had marijuana brought in, turning-on patients, and not conforming to hospital rules.

Unfortunately, Billy Bulka's responses to the interview questions and his views of life and death are not unique. They are echoed over and over again in the interviews with people ranked lowest on the self-actualization dimension. His interview is of special interest because every single response conforms to the model of the social dropout: he hangs on to a past he wishes he could undo; he shuns a future that is, at best, nonexistent; he knows that he will die prematurely, much sooner than he wants to. This ambivalence is most typical in suicidal cases. On the one hand, he longs for a normal life span and a natural death at the age of sixty or seventy. He wants to hold on to life, wishing he could come back a week after he dies or even sooner. But at the same time, he has always been courting death. His response to the fear of death question is also of special interest. He is fully aware that "there is *nothing* to stop it [death]—nothing that we can do." One may be tempted to conclude that the inevitability of death and his lack of control over it was so unbearable that suicide became his only defense against the intolerable experience of utter helplessness. I do not think, however, that this was the decisive factor in Billy's case. Rather, he committed suicide because life was even worse than death. He did not want to let go of it, but at the same time he could not go on with it. Undercutting his dreams and schemes with regrets of the past, he was seesawing between experiencing death as worse than life and life as worse than death. Neither was "good."

What made Bulka commit suicide while most others in similar situations will not do so? Perhaps his grandiose fantasies. He tells us immediately that he would like to create something that is *big* and *good*. His get-rich-quick schemes, like the kidnaping one, showed how much he lived in a fantasy world. He was very aware of his assets: his strength and his good looks. In some ways he felt superior to others, yet he evaluated everyone's situation as more advantageous than his own. But he did not envy them; the idea of a normal, unadventurous life held no appeal.

The question of choosing a period in which to live had, unfortunately, not been a part of the Standard Interview and was not presented to all participants. But whenever the question was asked (as typified in Bulka's interview) only the least self-actualized individuals would choose a period other than their own. While highly self-actualized people seem comfortable with their lives, unfulfilled people display a restlessness to consider another time—in the past or the future. All that matters is to avoid their own time and what they view as the failure of their lives.

The Bovinomorphic Fallacy[2]

Michael Hart

Michael Hart is a fifty-four-year-old stock broker. The interview took place at his estate in Westchester.

I.: What is the highest goal you would like to achieve?

M.H.: At this stage of my life, all I want is to maintain the status quo. I have a happy family life—I just don't want anything to change. If you had asked me twenty years ago, it was a different matter. I had more materialistic goals and idealistic ones as well. But I have attained the material ones and I have become rather skeptical on other fronts. I also feel that there is not enough time left to throw myself into any new ventures or undertake new projects.

I.: Were you ready to make great sacrifices to attain your goals?

M.H.: I can't say. I was very lucky; I never had to make great sacrifices. Well, that's not quite true. There were some things we would have liked to do and didn't, for financial reasons. We could have spent every penny I made, instead of making some good investments.

I.: Are you predominantly past, present, or future oriented?

M.H.: I suppose I am very past-oriented, even though I enjoy the present. But things will never be the same again. That whole era is gone. And I am not speaking about the real, deep values and ideals. Perhaps they don't change. What's gone is something I call "graciousness" and part of it is taste and tact. Life was certainly more exciting. I wished I could relive my life again.

[2]This is the bovinomorphic fallacy: Contentment is the ideal state of a cow on a green pasture. However, it is quite conceivable that a human being's ideal state is a different one.

I.: What about the future?

M.H.: I don't like to think about the future. It makes me tense. Of course, in my profession I am very future-oriented. I am constantly projecting. But that's different.

I.: Why does the future make you tense?

M.H.: I am not sure. Perhaps because there isn't much left of it. It's shrinking rapidly.

I.: How long do you expect to live?

M.H.: I have no expectations. When I referred to the future as "shrinking rapidly" I didn't mean to imply that I feel death is imminent. I thought of it in relation to my entire life span. I don't have another fifty-four years left. But I do think it's still far off.

I.: What is your preference, regarding the time of your death?

M.H.: I would like to reach old age.

I.: If after you died you could come back once for a short period of time, when would you choose to come back: 2, 10, 100, or 1,000 years after your death?

M.H.: A hundred years. I wouldn't want to look at people I now know. If I love them, it would be too painful, and if I don't, it's not interesting.

I.: If you could visit a past period, which one would you choose: two to ten years before your birth, 1900, 1700 to 1900, antiquity, or any other?

M.H.: The turn of the century. Before the First World War. I am not interested in old civilizations. I would like to see my parents' era.

I.: Are you afraid of death?

M.H.: I don't think so. I haven't had any close contact with it. I haven't suffered the death of anyone extremely close to me. It doesn't seem real enough to fear it.

I.: How often do you think about your own death?

M.H.: I don't. Hardly ever.

I.: Do you think you could sacrifice your life for anything; for a person or for a cause?

M.H.: Perhaps for a person. Not for a cause.

I.: If you knew you had only one year to live, would you make any changes in your life-style?

M.H.: Very few. I would probably make sure that all my things are in order and perhaps work less.

I.: Would you prefer to survive your wife or be survived by her?

M.H.: I have thought about that, occasionally. I hate both alternatives. But if I had to choose, I would opt to survive. I can't think of leaving her alone here. I always have taken care of her.

I.: If you could have chosen a period in which to live your life, would you have chosen a period in the past, the future, or your own?

M.H.: This may sound contradictory of what I had said about the past, but I would certainly choose my own period.

Tom Morse

Tom Morse is a forty-eight-year-old chemistry professor at a state college.

T.M.: I cannot speak of one ultimate goal. My life is meaningful to me and I want it to remain so. I want to achieve a certain level of functioning and live the kind of life that suits me.

I.: Can you be more specific on both counts?

T.M.: I'll try. Professionally, I know I will not set the world on fire—I won't win a Nobel Prize. But I like teaching, I like doing research, and I want to go on doing it. I want to have the feeling that I am increasing understanding—my own and that of my students. But there are so many other things I also like doing. I like to travel, I like to go skiing; I want to move out of the city, get a house in the country, and so on. All of these are goals. As soon as I reach one, another one takes its place.

I.: How much would you be willing to sacrifice to attain your goals?

T.M.: I don't know if I can answer that. You see, realistically, I know that no matter what I do, there are certain things I will never achieve. Now, if you could *guarantee* that I will reach all my goals if I made great sacrifices, well, there isn't anything I wouldn't do.

I.: What do you mean by "anything I wouldn't do"?

T.M.: Whatever necessary: work very hard, forgo vacations, save money—I love to spend it—whatever necessary.

I.: How about prostituting yourself? Getting yourself castrated or giving up years of your life?

T.M.: Physical prostitution, no. Not for anything. But that isn't really a choice; even if I were willing, I couldn't do it anyway. Moral prostitution? I can't say in the abstract. It depends on the issues involved and on the degree. Castration? No, absolutely not! I would rather sacrifice some years of my life, but I can't answer that one either.

I.: So the sacrifices you would be willing to make are in terms of work and some abstinences. And at that only with a "guarantee" that they will not be made in vain.

T.M.: That's right.

I.: What is your dominant time orientation: present, past, or future?

T.M.: The present. The present more than the future and the future more than the past.

I.: How long do you *expect* to live?

T.M.: A long time. Into old age.

I.: What is your *preference,* in terms of longevity?

T.M.: The same. I want to be around as long as possible.

I.: If after you died you could come back once for a short period of time, when would you choose to come back: 2, 10, 100, or 1,000 years after your death?

T.M.: That's a difficult decision. That is, two years and a thousand years I can rule out immediately. That's not interesting. I can interpolate what it's going to be like in two years—I don't anticipate any interesting changes, and a thousand years is much too far off; it has nothing to do with this life, as I know it. But ten years is of great *personal* interest: seeing how my family is doing, my students, my friends—and also issues I have been involved with: the environment, politics, art, etc. A hundred years would be more interesting, from a more *objective* standpoint. I would probably still be able to understand what's going on, but the changes would be dramatic, if we can judge from the changes that occurred in the last 100 years.

I.: Well, if you had to make a choice, would it be 10 or 100 years?

T.M.: I hate to say it, but if I am absolutely honest I would have to say 10 years.

I.: Why the reluctance?

T.M.: It seems somehow more broadminded to have a larger perspective. There is something "narrow" about sticking to the more personal interests, even beyond the grave.

I.: If you could visit a past period, which one would you choose: two to ten years before your birth, 1900, 1700 to 1900, antiquity, or any other?

T.M.: The early 1900s. Sounds like a very "civilized" time.

I.: Are you afraid of death?

T.M.: No. I don't think so. I would hate to die now, when there are still so many things I want to do, but I don't think about it. I am too preoccupied with life to worry about death.

I.: How often do you think about your death: daily, once a week, once a month, hardly ever?

T.M.: Hardly ever.

I.: If you could have chosen a period in which to live, would you have preferred a period in the past, the future, or your own?

T.M.: My own.

I.: If you knew that you had only one year to live, would you make any changes?

T.M.: Yes. Write my magnum opus, beget children, make some great discovery, see the pyramids, and the great wall of China. That would be great! Almost worthwhile to die afterwards. But seriously, I don't think I would make any changes.

The last two interviews are highly representative of those conducted with relatively successful people. Both Mr. Hart and Mr. Morse are well-functioning individuals who obviously like what they do. Though the knowledge of having to die does not seem to propel them toward unique accomplishment, neither does it appear to inhibit them from leading satisfying lives. Yet something *is* missing from both of these lives.

Let us compare Michael Hart's attitude toward life and death with those of Wheeler, Milstein, Stern, Gruber—all very much his senior (with the exception of Gruber). We find the latter four in the midst of challenges, struggles, and possible conquests; they are in the stream of life while Hart is carefully holding on to the safety of the river bank for fear of being swept away. He has reached his destination. In fact, perhaps thirty years before his death he seems to have prematurely reached the end in terms of change and growth, in terms of self-actualization.

Well, what is wrong with this as long as he is content? Perhaps

Hart's problem, which he shares with so many individuals is that very contentment—the bovinomorphic fallacy. He seems to be almost consciously holding back from any movement into the future, saying "there is not enough time left to throw myself into new ventures . . . " What does this really mean? Hart's condition is somewhat akin to that of a man who sits in his livingroom, waiting for a guest to arrive; he does not want to start any activity for fear of being interrupted. Only here the guest is death and Hart may have to wait for it for a long time. Perhaps this is why thinking about the future makes him feel tense.

Tom Morse's interview almost fits in with those of our highly creative group. Almost. It has some of their flavor but lacks the self-confidence that accompanies professional excellence, the intrinsic motivation and the broad time perspective. He, too, is holding back, but for reasons different from Hart's; he is unsure of his capabilities and he is bent on avoiding failure. If his success could only be guaranteed, he would lead a different kind of life. This statement succinctly points up one of the most important differences between truly creative individuals and all others. The former need no assurances. They have no choice but to pursue their activity wherever it may lead. The latter, on the other hand, deliberate whether it is worthwhile to do or not to do—and end up with mediocrity instead of greatness. To use Graham's words again, "There are no limits. Whatever you really want, you must want it irrationally."

Morse's response to the question dealing with a return visit after death is most interesting. After considering every alternative, he chooses the one given by the majority of all people interviewed, even though he is fully aware of its implications.[3] His reaction to the prospect of having only one year to live is also significant. Though he is intentionally facetious when he names all the things he would like to accomplish before his death, he admits in all earnestness that he would hate to die now with so many things left undone. We detect less than contentment. Morse is *not* trying to maintain the status quo. Thus, there is still hope. But hope for what?

There is no question that Morse as well as Hart lead far more fulfilling lives than Christian Bart, Steven Burek, or Harry Pitt. But

---

[3] I have frequently observed that the need *not* to deny one's own personality—to be true to oneself—is stronger than the need to respond in the most socially desirable way.

when compared to those of truly creative lives, theirs too appear impoverished. Yet to base these differences solely on the availability of potentials or talents is oversimplified. We have noted above that both Hart and Morse seem to be holding back from ventures into new territory—that is, into the future—for reasons other than a lack of possibilities. It may very well be that self-fulfillment depends as much on one's attitudes—on the way one regards one's life—as on talents. Perhaps the potential for unique accomplishment and self-fulfillment is present in most people, but certain attitudes toward life and death are also needed to actualize them. Of course, one could also argue that only those with extraordinary talents develop attitudes that allow them to lead self-actualizing lives.

Let us see what benefits we reap by choosing to implicate "bad attitudes" rather than "scanty potentials" as the cause of unfulfillment in so many. For one thing, we may be able to do something about changing attitudes, while there is very little we can do about increasing potentials. In fact, those potentials will most probably not be actualized fully anyway.

If Morse were to view *striving* toward his goals as more important than his ability to reach them, he would not need any guarantees. He would throw himself wholeheartedly into writing his magnum opus, begetting children, discovering the chemical essences of an insoluble compound, exploring the pyramids and the great wall of China. The fact that all these nonactualized possibilities come to his mind at the prospect of having only one year to live suggests that he is not stultified into contentment or hopelessness. Thus, there is still hope for growth and change, hope that when he dies, he may be "pointed in his chosen direction struggling to get there," to paraphrase Joe North.

Judging from the interviews, most *successful* people, who, however, lack that very special "creative spark," espouse attitudes toward life and death which resemble those of Hart and Morse. But even they constitute a small minority. By far the majority of *all* the people we interviewed echoed the frustrations, failures, and hopelessness that was expressed by Bart, Burek, Pitt, and Bulka.

Clearly, then, there exists a hierarchy based on the degree to which an individual has come to terms with death, which, in turn, corresponds to one's level of self-actualization. Although no one seems to be immune to a feeling of aversion at the prospect of death,

highly creative people deal more effectively with their fears and anxieties. As we step down the ladder of self-actualization, acknowledgment of one's finiteness becomes successively more intolerable. Clini-
cally, we note the increasing use and greater rigidity of defense
mechanisms, from sublimation and mild forms of intellectualization or
rationalization (used primarily by the artists and scientists) to ever
more exaggerated forms of repression, denial, and symptom formation, such as alcoholism and drug addiction.[4] The individual is caught
in a "cycle of despair": Apprehension about death, which leads to an
ever greater reliance on defense mechanisms, impedes self-
actualization and lack of self-actualization impedes the effort to come
to terms with death. This circular relationship is highly resistant to
change, since every aspect of it needs to be changed *first*. This may
explain our compulsion for repeating the same self-defeating patterns
of behavior over and over again. It is a trap only a few escape from.

---

[4]Even the most severe psychotic reaction is held to be a defense against the intolerable
fear of death.

III

Winning
the Race
with Death

9

Self-fulfillment or Immortality

Why, like a well-filled guest, not leave the feast of life?

—Lucretius

Can the race with death be won? Only if life can be brought to completion by actualizing and exhausting all one's potentials. However, if these potentials are infinitely renewable, we would do better to shoot for immortality.

There was no consensus among the artists and scientists interviewed as to whether human potentials were self-generating; nor was there agreement as to the desirability of a finite existence. Howard Gruber most explicitly challenged the assumption that mental potentials are limited and must eventually become exhausted. He views the individual as an open system capable of regenerating itself indefinitely as long as the physical functions remain intact. Though he recognizes the inevitable loss of energy which sets limits on physical functions, he treats mental exhaustion as an epiphenomenon of the physical one summarized in his retort "If my flesh doesn't weaken, my mind won't." Pribram and Bernstein share Gruber's view of the individual life as an open system with "bottomless mental potential," as Bernstein expressed it, and with an infinite capacity for continued intellectual growth.

The wish to banish death is certainly consistent with a conception that precludes the possibility of ever completing life. Yet there was no consensus—even among those who believe in the inexhaustability of potentials—as to whether or not to keep death alive. Those, however, who view human potential as finite rather than infinite, capable of being fully actualized and eventually used up, agree with Margenau when he says, "I have reached my goals. . . . It would be terribly boring to live forever. . . . In my philosophy, a finite life is the desirable thing."

The controversy is not a new one. In literature we frequently find death personified arguing in favor of mortality. In *The Plowman and Death* (Von Tepl, 1957), Death makes an impassioned speech in its own defense:

> Had we not exterminated the new growth and the multiplication of man on earth, of animals and worms in the wilderness and on the open heath, of scale-bearing and of slippery fishes in the sea, since the time of the first man—made of clay—no one could have endured for [the plight of] small insects, no one would dare into the open for [the fear of] wolves. Man would devour man, animal devour animal, all living beings would destroy each other for lack of food, for lack of space on this earth.
>
> Foolish is he who bemoans the death of mortals. [Author's translation].

Montaigne, too, comes to the defense of death. And paraphrasing Seneca and Lucretius, he lets Nature argue the virtues of death: "Make room for others, as others have for you," and:

> Chiron refused immortality when informed of its condition by the very god of time and duration, his father Saturn. Imagine honestly how much less bearable and more painful to man would be an everlasting life than the life I gave him. If you did not have death, you would curse me incessantly for having deprived you of it.
>
> Death is the condition of your creation, it is part of you; you are fleeing from your own selves. This being of yours that you enjoy is equally divided between death and life. The first day of your birth leads you towards death as towards life.

On the other hand, Goethe, like some of our present-day artists and scientists, would most certainly have opted for immortality, at least for himself. Much has been made of Goethe's death phobia. Indeed, death is the only major human problem he does not have much to say about—or so it seems, at least. He certainly did not want to be told when anyone close to him was dying, and if he did learn about it, as in the case of his long-time friend Christian von Voigt, he refused Voigt's request for a last encounter (Friedenthal, 1964). When his wife's sister, who lived in his home, became terminally ill and died, it was kept a secret from him until long after the funeral. And when his wife, Christiane, was dying—suffering two days of unmitigated agony—Goethe did not go into her room, before or after her death. Her body had to be removed immediately. Goethe had lived with her for almost three decades, and yet he did not attend the funeral (Friedenthal, 1964).

Nevertheless, the problems of human potential, of striving toward self-fulfillment, and that of immortality were very much on his mind. Thus, reflecting on the early deaths of Mozart, Schubert, and Weber, he remarked to Eckermann (1955), "They all had to get 'wrecked.' They had fulfilled their mission. They had to make way, so that others will have things left to be done, in a world programmed to endure a long time." But he had no intention to make room for others, since his own mission seemed endless: "I would not know what to do with eternal blessedness, if it didn't offer new problems and challenges to conquer. But we have only to look at the planets and the sun, to be reminded that there will be enough 'nuts to crack.'" Thus, he is telling us, very much like Wheeler and Gruber and so many others, that he is not going to run out of projects. But Goethe goes a step further. He is "owed" self-actualization. He tells Eckermann that he is convinced of his "continuation": "If I function effectively and unceasingly until my death, it is incumbent upon nature to supply me with another life-supporting form, if the present one can no longer sustain my mind" (Author's translation).

When Goethe contemplates "eternal blessedness" or "continuation" it is not meant in a religious sense, even though he conceives of it as an after-death state of being. It is certainly not the Christian Kingdom of Heaven, which he sarcastically assigned only to "those who did not make out well here on earth." But science had not acquired the omnipotent status it occupies today. Thus, he could hardly contemplate the possibility of survival by banishing death altogether, or at least long enough to "sustain his active mind." The problem of immortality and afterlife were, indeed, very much on his mind. He tells Friedrich von Müller that he cannot fathom the cessation of thinking nor the cessation of life; but that as soon as one attempts to prove dogmatically the necessity of one's own continuation, one loses oneself in contradictions; nevertheless, man is driven to attempt an alliance with the impossible. More than that, he views almost all laws of nature as "syntheses of impossibilities" (Friedenthal, 1964). But for Goethe this is just as it should be: the only way to reach the utmost possible is by pursuing the impossible. And it is this very pursuit which he viewed as man's noblest feature. Since neither science nor religion held the solution to the utterly unacceptable prospect of death, Goethe looked for it elsewhere. He thought he had found it in the "activity principle," which holds as its essence man's infinite striving toward ever higher peaks. And that is what Faust is all about: the restless striving, at all cost, toward the actualization of all human possibilities, nay, impossibilities—even if it demands a pact with the devil. And the reward for such striving? Salvation! (Whatever that means to Goethe.) The devil is cheated of his bounty (though he fulfilled his part of the bargain) and the angels, carrying the *immortal* part of Faust, sing:

> Him can we save that tireless strove
> Ever to higher level.

On several occasions reference was made to living beings as open systems. Of course all living organisms are by definition open systems. There are, however, degrees of openness. When we conceive of the individual as possessing infinite regenerative powers, extreme openness is implied, while a relatively closed system is presumably limited to predetermined quanta of energy exchange. With all his ideas of infinite continuation and renewal, Goethe views man as an "entelechy"—an entity striving toward a fixed end-state, which is the full realization of its form-giving cause. Thus, the end is predetermined from the beginning, indicating a relatively closed system. Goethe's position is clearly a vitalistic one, in tune with eighteenth century views of science.

Ehrenberg's (1946) system, too, is predominantly a closed one, though he refutes all vitalistic notions of man as much as he refutes machine theories. We shall present his theoretical position in some detail, since it represents a scientifically tenable view of life as "completable."

Death is the very core of life. It is not only inevitable, not just a consequence of organic processes or the running-down of the organic machinery, but an absolute necessity for life. Life is a course[1] and its flow, its one-directional pulling force, is death. The law of necessity of death is a biological analogy of the physical law of entropy. And just like the latter, it applies only to relatively closed systems. Though a biological system can never be strictly closed spatially, it is a spatial–temporal closed system. That is, it turns to an ever more closed system, and this very process is the course of all life, be it that of a cell, a culture of microbes, or a human being.

All *self-maintaining* processes in nature need a source of energy, which diminishes in accordance with the progression of the process. In physics this refers to free or potential energy which diminishes as it is converted into "bound" or "depreciated" energy. Since the process is never fully reversible, Ehrenberg applies this observation, taken from thermodynamics, to life: If one can speak of depreciated energy, its opposite, usable energy, must be energy that is free, that can be utilized; it must possess inherent possibilities capable of having effects. But in the course of life the possibility of progress in the system decreases simultaneously with the progress—as the potential resources (free energy) are converted into structures. On the organic level, structure includes all substance which changes from a soluble, free state into a solid or fixed state and is irreversible without radical intervention. On the functional level, every psychological event, every experience, is a structure with the same irreversibility to its former undeveloped potential. Thus, death occupies the same position as absolute zero in thermodynamics.

It is not the law of entropy, however, that condemns living organisms to death. The crucial question is not how much free energy is available, but how much room is there to take it in. Comparing a living system to the lower part of an hourglass, its function is completed when it is *full*—regardless of the resources still left in the upper part. It is the process of filling up that sets the time limit of life. It also turns the relatively open system into a progressively more closed system. Possibilities decrease with increased actualization. The state that is richest in yet unrealized possibilities is the most vital one, while the most actualized one is death. But the essence of all life processes is

[1]Ehrenberg uses the German *Lebensablauf,* connoting a downward flowing course, the unwinding or unrolling of life, whose direction cannot be reversed.

the realization of possibilities, that is, the conversion of unstructured into structured. To the degree that structures are irreversible, they inhibit further life processes. Thus, the impediments are not by-products of life, not waste products; they are the developing and the developed structures. The essence of life itself is its own impediment. Its end is in the truest sense of the word its completion, its fulfillment. Life is fulfilled in the process of filling itself.

Ehrenberg takes exception to the analogy between the course of life and the diurnal course of the sun: from morning through noon to evening; or seen as a curve: childhood and youth, maturity, old age paralleling ascent, horizontal extension, descent, respectively. Their inherent value bias for youth against old age is incompatible with a view of constant growth in complexity and individuality as life processes strive toward completion. The fallacy of life curving downward is widespread ("Whom the gods love they let die young") but biologically and biographically unfounded: there is a path, a constant progression leading through the *whole* course of life, and through it life becomes truly the fulfillment of time. A highly optimistic view!

Whether or not one agrees with Ehrenberg's theoretical position, his Principle of Structurization and the Law of the Necessity of Death are of great heuristic value, helping to explain some of the recurring themes in the interviews with creative people and in looking at creative lives from a new perspective. Thus, we find that striving toward higher levels of development—artistic, scholastic, or personal—finds expression in almost every interview. Stern is still searching, Milstein changing; Arkin speaks of reaching freedom from self-involvement; Tobey seeks to increase understanding as Wheeler strives to find meaning, and Graham pushes toward the unknown—and so it goes. Clearly, the hallmark of creative life is the pull from the future and the freedom and courage to follow it.

But there is a second theme occurring somewhat less frequently and more exclusively in the interviews with creative people: the closer one comes to reaching whatever one is striving for, the greater the experience of completion or fulfillment. The parallel to Ehrenberg's Principle of Structurization—approaching completion (death) as unstructured is converted into structured—is striking. The feeling was most explicitly expressed in responses to the fear-of-death question. Alan Arkin: "Since I have done my thing, I am no longer afraid of death." Lyman Spitzer: "If one has done what one has been equipped to do, one can die." Ronald Graham: " . . . if one has *lived*, one can die." Herman A. Witkin (shortly before his death): " . . . I have fulfilled myself. I have no fear." Interestingly, even Gruber, who does not believe that we can ever actualize our potentials to the point of experiencing fulfillment, did say, " . . . if I have to die, at least my kids are grown up, at least I did get the Darwin book out. I did make one kind of unique statement personally, and another kind of unique statement professionally. . . . If I were to die tomorrow I would be a little less disappointed because of that."

What these statements are saying is that it is easier to die once one has lived. They also affirm that life is meaningful. There is certainly nothing that sounds strange in these statements—common sense tells us as much even without the interviews; it is strange, however, that these positive views of one's own life and of death are the exception, not the rule. We might have expected the relatively healthy, vigorous view of the human condition held by the highly creative; it is the rather defeatist view held by the vast majority that comes as a surprise.

To assert in the face of death, "I have fulfilled myself, I can die," certainly takes the sting out of that fateful final hour. But even more important, to know that one is doing all that one is equipped to do, to experience life as meaningful while one is still in the midst of it, may well take the sting out of death and liberate us from the fear that inhibits most people to strive toward self-actualization in the first place.

The question remains: Can that view be changed?.

10

A New Vision

When a person is young he dates time from the beginning of his existence, and when he's older, he dates time from when his existence will end. And there's a feeling that time is precious—that every day is a gift.

—*John A. Wheeler*

In the few hundred interviews that I conducted in preparation for writing this book, I have encountered some ambivalence and an overwhelming amount of apprehension about death; but hardly a case of total equanimity—let alone joy—at the thought of one's mortality. The prospect of death has indeed a tremendous effect on all creative endeavor. At one extreme, it acts as the great motivator, the very source of all achievement; at the other extreme, it inhibits all self-actualizing activity.

The *prospect* of death need not be synonymous with apprehension about death. Apprehension enslaves people by keeping them chained to their defense mechanisms; yet indifference may well remove the necessary pull toward self-actualization. There may be an optimal way in the lifelong process of approaching death: a way that would allow us to experience the human condition as meaningful rather than absurd; life as fulfilling and terminable rather than frustrating and incomplete; death as an ultimate goal, worth striving for, rather than a lifelong threat to dash our hopes. Such as alternative view of the human condition necessitates first of all a completely new approach to our perception of time. Ehrenberg has taken such an approach. In accordance with his Principle of Structurization, the age of an organism is measured by the amount of potential still available to it in order to carry on life processes. Age is not measured from birth, but backward from death to the present. In discussing Ehrenberg's theoretical framework, Kurt Eissler (1955) remarked:

The question, then, would not be how long *has* he lived but how long *can* he live. The felicity of this approach is striking. Man is not, or at least should not be, interested in how much of life has passed, but only in how much he still has to live. . . . How much structurization is this person still capable of?

Ehrenberg's age assessment represents a shift from a past time perspective to a future one. It requires a total reorientation toward life, aging, and death—and this at the beginning of life, rather than at the end of it. Ehrenberg's formulation abolishes the arbitrary dichotomy between the "living" and the "dying." Indeed, it equates death with the completion of life, the ultimate goal we are *actively* striving to reach, rather than the dreaded event we will inevitably have to endure.

Although the merit of Ehrenberg's principle has received some recognition on theoretical grounds, no one has ever ventured seriously to discuss ways in which Ehrenberg's age assessment could be implemented. And for good reason! Whenever we visualize future possibilities, whenever we advocate changes and try to anticipate the consequences of these changes, we venture into an untested domain that exists only in our imagination. We are afraid of sounding utopian, unrealistic, mystical, or, at best, like a science fiction writer. Aside from suspicion and skepticism, our response to making fundamental changes is a spontaneous, almost reflex-like rejection: "If it were superior to our present ways, human beings would have adopted it long ago"—implying that our present condition is the best possible one.

But besides this natural resistance, a general shift in time perspective may well be beyond the human repertoire. Nevertheless, we shall take the risk and follow Ehrenberg's view to its logical conclusion.

To measure age by one's distance from death requires an estimate of the time of death. It is conceivable that we will be able to extract a rough longevity estimate from a matrix of genetic, physiological, psychological, and environmental factors. This estimate, calculated at birth and revised at various stages throughout life, would keep us informed of our age, that is, of how much time we still have ahead of us. To put it more dramatically, each person would have a "death-day" (D-Day) or, if you prefer, a "completion" or a "fulfillment-day." Sounds depressing so far? Perhaps it need not be. An individual's life would not be a day shorter because of D-Day, just as we do not live an hour longer by not knowing when we are going to die. It also would not mean that there will be an execution day any more than there is now. But by way of this reorientation we might expect a difference in the way that we anticipate death.

One may object to Ehrenberg's age assessment on methodological grounds:

1. Measuring age from birth (or conception) is universal and applicable to all living organisms including plants and animals as well as mountains, planets, and anything else that has a determinable beginning. We have objective units of measurement which allow us to make comparisons and to formulate laws. The problem with our traditional method of measuring, however, lies in its very generality: with the same units of time used to measure the speed of light, the age of an antique chair, and the chronology of a person's life, the individual human being finds the meaning and validity of such measurement limited. What do we really measure? Nothing more than the number of years that someone has been around since birth.

2. Assessing age by future potential can never be as accurate as measuring it by the organism's past trajectory. Undoubtedly true! But what is the purpose of our assessment? Should we concern ourselves primarily with precision, regardless of whether or not the implications resulting from our measurement do justice to the object we are measuring? This presents the old dilemma of favoring precision or relevance. We can be very precise as to how long someone has been around, but it may not be relevant at all to the individual's most vital problem: how much time remains to complete her or his life? Our present age assessment determines quantity while Ehrenberg's dimension includes something of its quality.

3. Potential longevity may never coincide with an individual's actual time of death. Thus, postulating a "death-day" would not remove our present uncertainty; we may never reach it or we may live beyond it.

Indeed, we may never refine our longevity assessment to the point of narrowing it down to a single day. We may succeed in rough estimates, periodically revised, of a few years' span, similar to our present-day prognosis of the terminally ill. Eventually we may increase precision to a time span of a year or even to months. On theoretical grounds, living beyond the actualization of all our potentials, which is synonymous with both the completion of life and the depletion of life-sustaining capabilities, should be impossible. Yet dying before one reaches D-Day (that is, "premature death") could occur within Ehrenberg's framework of structurization. Thus, a person's death-day could be any arbitrarily chosen day within a limited time span, based on the best available estimate. But what advantage does postulating a death-day serve, especially since the psychological objections appear to be even stronger than the methodological ones?

The mere *idea* of knowing our death-day or that of our beloved—say, two years hence—evokes pangs of anxiety. Milstein's objections echo throughout the interview: "If I knew when I am going to die, I could no longer enjoy myself." No doubt, within our present context of existence, the sudden pinpointing of a rendezvous with death would startle us traumatically. And since all our present defenses rely most heavily on repression, which would become utterly useless—one can't face death and not face death simultaneously—anxiety could well be overwhelming. In psychotherapy it is a well-known axiom not to tear down a defensive structure, no matter how self-deceptive or energy-consuming, before replacing it with a more effective tool. This axiom certainly applies when we consider a reorientation toward death. We need a new context in which to view our entire life before we can properly evaluate a change in any one of its facets.

Interestingly, we found that people who have thought a great deal about death and are intimately aware of their finiteness most likely favor a foreknowledge of the time of their death. The well-known "physician syndrome" seems relevant here: though most physicians claim that they would want to know the truth if they were terminally ill, they believe that their patients would prefer not to know (Gorer, 1956; Feifel, 1965).

Intuitively, "knowing" seems superior to "not knowing," wherever that knowledge may lead. In the case of our longevity, we may find our resistance especially difficult to understand since the available evidence points to a dramatic enhancement of the value of life when one increases awareness of its time limitation. I do not know whether most people subscribe to the age-old wisdom that ignorance is bliss, but we act as if it were so. But we can pretend that ignorance is bliss only as long as we or those we love are not terminally ill or otherwise at a stage in life which we now label "dying." When that happens, we are totally unprepared to deal with it. Thus, the death of a person close to us is not only a most traumatic event, it is frequently also a fatal one. The percentage of bereaved dying within a year of the death of a spouse is extraordinarily high, while innumerable parents' lives are utterly destroyed by the death of their child. Kübler-Ross (1971) has discussed the salutary effect of preparatory grief—grieving for some-one who is dying through weeks, months, or even years of her or his terminal illness. In these cases the trauma at the time of death might be lessened. But there are some who experience "enlightened prepara-tory grief" throughout life—not as a trauma—not even as a lessening of the *joie de vivre*. On the contrary, by intensifying our awareness of the ephemeral, it ennobles and deepens our relationships, making our lives all the more precious.

Attempts to shelve death are not too successful anyway as a little exercise in introspection will surely reveal: whenever we say to another person, "I love you"—not frivolously, not playfully but dead-seriously—it always has a touch of the tragic, an intimation of death. And the great esthetic experiences do not produce mirth but awe, carrying with them an intimation of death.

It is again the poet who expresses these feelings most eloquently. In the following lines Death reminds us of its presence in all the truly great moments in life:

> When in the mild mid-summer eve
> A leaf drifted down through golden air
> My breath, fluttering dreamlike around ripe things,
> Caused you to shudder.
> When swamped with feelings
> The trembling soul is filled,
> When in a sudden flash
> The mysterious reveals itself as kindred,
> And you, surrendering to that great sway,
> Received the world as your own:
> In every truly great hour,
> Which made you tremble,
> I have touched the depth of your soul
> With awesome, secret might.

[Hofmannsthal, 1970. Author's translation]

Death is there, but we need to tune in on it if we are to live life to the fullest while there is still time. The recognition of the fleeting or, as the god Jupiter expressed it in Giraudoux's *Amphitryon 38*, the "poignance of the transient—the intimation of mortality—that sweet sadness at grasping at something you cannot hold . . . " manifests itself as "enlightened preparatory grief," endowing each day with a preciousness that may well be envied by the immortal gods. (At least, Jupiter tells us so.)

Let us now imagine that we postulated death-days, and that at the time of forming a close bond between two people we knew the longevity of each partner. To make it even more concrete, suppose that at the time of our marriage, our mate's estimated death-day was thirty years hence, and our own fifty years hence. Thus, we prepare ourselves from the onset to the prospect of spending thirty years together and twenty years alone (provided that "only death do us part"). The practical advantages of having to face the situation, of being almost forced to plan a *whole* life accordingly, are immediately obvious: career decisions, financial provisions, geographic-residential choices to name only a few. But much more important are the psychological ramifications that a more accurate knowledge of our time limitation would have.

One of the most devastating consequences of our present unawareness of our limited timespan are the regrets—most bitter regrets—of all the things we did or did not do, of all the unspoken words we had wanted to utter which must forever remain unsaid; the regrets of thoughts and feelings and of time not shared with one another; the regrets of having let great moments slip by without realizing that each of them alone could have made living and dying worthwhile. Too often do we hear the sorrowful complaint of the dying or the bereaved: "Had I only known! I never would have . . . !" But there is no making up once death intervenes. No making up can occur in the last hour, the last month, the last year for a lifetime of missed opportunities. It may sound contradictory, but only when death is an intimate part of our lives—a constant presence—do we no longer live in its shadow; only when every moment in life becomes as important as the last moment do we truly live life to the fullest. I think that the most traumatic events of our lives are immensely more bearable when we eliminate regret.

In a lighter vein, death-days serving as constant reminders of the transient nature of our voyage through life may very well change our attitudes toward our fellow travelers. Somehow we seem more vulnerable when our days are numbered (even when the number leaps into the tens of thousands). Would we not be more protective, more patient toward those around us if we knew that their days are numbered, too? As Shaw remarked, "All is well that ends."

Other benefits accrue when we postulate death-days. As a hedonistic society, we have neglected death because of our failure to turn it into a pleasurable event. Death-day can accomplish just that: the climactic celebration of the culmination of life.

An important aspect of a new vision of the human condition involves the celebration of death rather than its mourning. If, from earliest childhood on, our projected death-day symbolized the completion of life, we could experience death as the ultimate goal we strive to reach. By actively participating in our destiny, death would no longer represent an inevitable fate over which we have no control. We could convert the most dreaded event which haunts us throughout our lives into the crowning achievement: having reached self-fulfillment. Thus, the celebration of death-day would represent a complete reversal of our present attitude toward death. One need not conceive of death-day mystically, nor consider this a glorification of death. On the contrary, our purpose should be to glorify life—a race against death—which we can win by completing life, by experiencing self-fulfillment.

And what about those who win the race with death and linger a while after celebrating D-Day? Let us leave it to the reader's imagination to devise ways in which an enlightened, humanistic civilization—freed from the traumatic fear of death—would celebrate and bestow privileges on the most venerable members of their society who have won the race with death.

The legacy we can leave behind is the satisfaction of our accomplishments—however private and personal—instead of regrets. Fear of death, we have seen, immobilizes us and maims the imagination; yet we cannot strive and realize our dreams until we squarely face the issue. Perhaps we now regard death as the nemesis who, at the moment of death, forces us to recall the inconclusive state of our lives, making us gaze back at the past, rather than seeing it as our state in the future—completion. Only when we switch perspectives will death seem less the bogeyman and more the friend.

As Ted Rosenthal reminded us, "I don't think people are afraid of death. What they are afraid of is the incompleteness of their life."

Bibliography

Alvarez, A. *The savage god*. Random House, New York, 1970.

Butler, R. N. The life review: an interpretation of reminiscence in the aged. *Psychiatry*, 1963, *119*, 721–728.

Dickstein, L. & Blatt, S. Death concern, futurity and anticipation. *Journal of Consulting Psychology*, 1966, *31*, 11–17.

Eckermann, Johann Peter. *Eckermanns Gespräche mit Goethe*. Fritz Bergemann, Wiesbaden, 1955.

Ehrenberg, Rudolf. *Theoretische Biologie*. Springer, Berlin, 1923.

———. *Leben und Tod*. C. Bertelsmann Verlag, Gütersloh, 1925.

———. *Der Lebensablauf*. Lambert Schneider, Heidelberg, 1946.

Eissler, Kurt, R. *The psychiatrist and the dying patient*. International University Press, New York, 1955.

Esfandiary, F. M. Sorry, we're here for eternity. *The New York Times*, September 24, 1974.

Feifel, Herman. Attitudes towards death in some normal and mentally ill populations. In H. Feifel (ed.), *The meaning of death*. McGraw-Hill, New York, 1959.

———. The functions of attitudes towards death. Group for the Advancement of Psychiatry: *Death and dying: attitudes of patient and doctor*. GAP Symposium, L II, Vol. 5, 1965, pp. 632–641.

Frankl, Viktor, E. *Man's search for meaning*. Washington Square Press, New York, 1971.

Freud, Sigmund. Thoughts for the times on war and death. *Collected Papers*, Vol. 4. (1915) Basic Books, New York, 1959.

———. *A general introduction to psychoanalysis*. (1915–1917) Washington Square Press, New York, 1960.

———. *Beyond the pleasure principle.* (1920) Bantam Books, New York, 1959.

———. The future of an illusion. In *The complete psychological works of Sigmund Freud.* (1927) Hogarth Press, London, 1961.

Friedenthal, Richard. *Goethe—Sein Leben und seine Zeit.* Piper & Co. Verlag, Munich, 1964.

Giraudoux, Jean. *Amphitryon 38* (S. N. Behrman adaptation). In Cerf and Cartmell (eds.), *Sixteen famous European plays.* The Modern Library, New York, 1943.

Goethe, Johann Wolfgang von. Faust 2. Teil. In *Goethe's sämmtliche Werke.* 2. Band. I. G. Cotta'scher Verlag, Stuttgart, 1858.

Goodman, L. Marburg. Attitudes towards death in creative artists. *Omega,* 1975, *6* (4).

———. Attitudes towards death as a function of age and level of accomplishment. 21st International Congress of Psychology, Paris, France, 1976.

Gorer, G. *Death, grief and mourning.* Doubleday (Anchor), New York, 1956.

Gruber, Howard E. "And the bush was not consumed." The evolving system approach to creativity. In Sohan and Celia Modgil (eds.), *Towards a theory of psychological development.* National Foundation for Educational Research, Windsor, England, 1979.

Heidegger, Martin. *Sein und Zeit: Erste Hälfte.* Max Niemeyer Verlag, Halle, 1927.

Hofmannsthal, Hugo von. *Der Tor und der Tod.* Insel Verlag, Frankfurt am Main, 1970.

Hölderlin, F. *An die Parzen* (To the fates). 1798.

Jung, Carl J. On psychic energy. *Collected works,* Vol. 8, Princeton University Press, Princeton, 1960.

Kastenbaum, Robert. Time and death in adolescence. In H. Feifel (ed.), *The meaning of death.* McGraw-Hill, New York, 1959.

———. & Aisenberg, R. *The psychology of death.* Springer, New York, 1972.

———. *Death, society and human experience.* Mosby, St. Louis, 1977.

Kaufmann, Walter. *Existentialism, religion and death.* New American Library, New York, 1976.

Keats, John. When I have fears that I may cease to be. In H. E. Scudder, (ed.), *Complete poetical works and letters.* Student's Cambridge Edition, Houghton Mifflin, 1899.

Kübler-Ross, Elisabeth. *Death and dying.* Macmillan, New York, 1971.

Lamont, R. The double apprenticeship: life and the process of dying. In E. Wyschorgrod (ed.), *The phenomenon of death.* Harper & Row, New York, 1973.

Lifton, Robert S. *Death in life*. Random House, New York, 1976.

Maddi, Salvatore R. Myth and personality. Symposium: *Personality, situation and motives in aesthetic production*. 86th Annual Convention, American Psychological Association, Toronto, 1978.

Marcuse, Herbert. The ideology of death. In H. Feifel (ed.), *The meaning of death*. McGraw-Hill, New York, 1959.

Montaigne, Michel de. That to philosophize is to learn to die. *The complete essays of Montaigne*. Stanford University Press, Palo Alto, California, 1965.

Nelson, B. The games of life and the dances of death. In E. Wyschorgrod (ed.), *The phenomenon of death*. Harper & Row, New York, 1973.

Rilke, Rainer Maria. Briefwechsel in Gedichten mit Erika Mitterer. *Aus Rainer Maria Rilke Nachlass, 2. Folge*. Insel, Wiesbaden, 1950.

Rosenthal, Ted. *How could I not be among you?* George Braziller, New York, 1973.

Rosner, S. & Abt, L. B. *The creative experience*. Grossman, New York, 1970.

Seiden, Henry. *Time perspectives and styles of consciousness*. Doctoral dissertation, New School for Social Research, 1969.

Shneidman, Edwin S. You and death. *Psychology Today*, June, 1971.

———. *Death of man*. Quadrangle/The New York Times Book Co., New York, 1973.

Simmel, Georg. Tod und Unsterblichkeit. In *Lebensanschauung: Vier Metaphysische Kapitel*. Duncker & Humbolt, Munich, Leipzig, 1918.

Spilka, Bernard. Some meanings and correlates of future time and death perspectives among college students. *Omega* 1970, *1*, 49–56.

Stuart, Jesse, *The year of my rebirth*. McGraw-Hill, New York, 1956.

Tepl, Johannes von. *Der Ackermann und der Tod* (1400). Insel-Verlag, Wiesbaden, 1957.

Tolstoy, Leon. *The death of Ivan Illyich* (1886). Health Science Publishing Corp., New York, 1973.

Toynbee, Arnold. *Man's concern with death*. McGraw-Hill, New York, 1969.

Wallace, M. Future time perspective in schizophrenia. *Journal Abnormal and Social Psychology*, 1956, *52*, 240–245.

Weisman, Avery D. *On dying and denying*. Behavioral Publication Inc., New York, 1972.

Index